GERMAN TANK DEVELOPMENT AFTER WORLD WAR II

On 9 May 1955 the Federal Republic of Germany (FDR) was admitted into the North Atlantic Treaty Organisation (NATO) joining the Alliance's original members, the United Kingdom, France, Belgium, the Netherlands, Luxembourg, Canada, Portugal, Italy, Norway, Denmark, Iceland and the United States. This led, just five days later, to the signing of the Treaty of Friendship, Cooperation and Mutual Assistance between the Soviet Union, Albania, Bulgaria, Czechoslovakia, East Germany, Hungary, Poland and Romania. The formation of the so-called Warsaw Pact marked the beginning of a new stage in the Cold War and one that transformed West Germany into the front line of the struggle between the two Superpowers.

West Germany's membership of NATO also presaged the creation of the Bundeswehr on 12 November 1955. This new force for the defence of West Germany had been planned by high-ranking German officers and the chancellor of the Federal Republic, Konrad Adenauer, since 1950. Its equipment was, at first, provided principally through an American Military Assistance Advisory Group and the armoured force of the Bundeswehr was initially equipped with American M47 and M48 Patton medium tanks and M41 Walker Bulldog light tanks. The Bundeswehr had, of course, a wealth of experience in armoured warfare and this, as well as the reluctance of other European countries to be dependent on American military aid, led to the creation in 1957 of the FINABEL military study group (comprising France, Italy, the Netherlands, Belgium and Luxembourg as well as the FDR). It was estimated that the Bundeswehr would require some 2,000 main battle tanks (MBTs) to equip the Panzerwaffe and defend the FDR against the armoured might of the Warsaw Pact. The existing American medium tanks were considered too heavy and lacking mobility and European tank designers called for more mobile armoured tactics.

LEOPARD 1

In 1957 the West Germans, Fre Italians decided to develop a c battle tank (FINABEL 3A5). The agreement specified a tank of some thirty tons, armed with a 105mm main gun and with high battlefield mobility resulting from a power to weight ratio of 30 HP/ton. Within a couple of years this project had run into difficulties, largely because of differences in national policy between France and West Germany, but the progress made eventually resulted in the French AMX-30 and German Leopard. The task of progressing the so-called Standard-Panzer to replace the M47 and M48 was given to two competing syndicates of West German heavy industrial companies, Warneke and Porsche. Each was responsible for a hull design that would carry a common turret design. Various main guns were considered, the Rheinmetall 105mm smoothbore, the French 105mm CN F1 and the British 105mm L7. After the Americans had chosen the L7, the Bundeswehr followed suit in adopting the British gun. Porsche's prototype was finally selected in 1963, principally for its simplicity. The prototype Leopard was a 37-ton tank armed with the British L7 105mm gun, a weapon which was being adopted as the NATO standard tank armament. Other features of the design were the use of a torsion bar suspension with seven roadwheels each side, as well as a ten-cylinder MTU diesel power pack.

The Bundeswehr purchased some 1,500 Leopard 1 vehicles with the original cast turret between 1965 and 1971 in four production batches. The first Leopards were delivered to the Bundeswehr between September 1965 and July 1966. The M48 tanks remained in service into the 1980s, upgraded with a 105mm gun, to serve alongside the Leopard 1, to provide the Bundeswehr time to build up its stock of MBTs. The original Leopard 1 were upgraded to Leopard 1A1 status with a turret appliqué armour package which was also sold to the Netherlands. This model also incorporated a gun-stabilisation

The M48 Patton, procured under the Military Assistance Program from the United States, was the mainstay of the Bundeswehr's tank forces until the deployment of the Leopard 1 and remained in service until the 1980s. (M.P. Robinson)

A Bundeswehr Leopard 1 (later renamed Leopard 1A1). The first production order of 1,400 vehicles was made in 1963. The original design was very simple in comparison to the variants that followed. (M.P. Robinson)

package that allowed the tank to fire on the move and the characteristic side skirts. The next major model was designated Leopard 1A2, fitted with a more heavily armoured turret, as well as, successively, an image intensification system (Leopard 1A2A1) and digital radios (Leopard 1A2A2). 232 were built between 1972 and 1974. A new welded turret was developed for the fifth series Leopard 1A3 (of which 110 were built) and the Leopard 1A4 that followed in 1974 (250 vehicles built) which employed welded spaced armour instead of cast homogeneous steel. The Leopard 1A3 and Leopard 1A4 dispensed with the optical rangefinder in favour of laser rangefinders, and the Leopard 1A4 was also fitted with an independent sighting system, the Peri R12. In 1980 the decision was taken to upgrade 1,225 older Leopard 1s to Leopard 1A5 standard with a new fire control system, a night-vision capability and a redesigned turret ammunition stowage. The tank was also adapted to fit additional bolt-on turret armour packages. These late model Leopards were also sold to Canada and Australia, where they continued to serve into the 21st century (seeing action in Afghanistan with the Canadians as the Leopard C2). In all some 2,400 Leopard 1 MBTs were produced, as well as numerous support vehicles including the Biber AVLB, Pioneerpanzer, Gepard Flakpanzer, and the Bergepanzer recovery vehicle.

The Leopard 1, for all its success as an upgradeable and flexible design in Bundeswehr service, was also a great export success within NATO. Belgium (1968), the Netherlands (1969), Norway (1970), Italy (1971 with a production license for 800 vehicles), Denmark (1976), Canada (1978), Turkey (1980) and Greece (1981) all purchased Leopard 1 MBTs to replace or supplement their Centurion, M47 and M48 fleets. The British Royal Armoured Corps had also evaluated two Leopard prototypes in comparative trials to their own Chieftain in the early 1960s. The Leopard 1 was undoubtedly the most successful MBT of the 1960s, outperforming and outselling its rivals, the AMX-30 and the Vickers 37-ton tank adopted by India as the Vijayanta. Its relative simplicity, however, meant that it was not sophisticated enough to outclass the new generation of Soviet tanks, the T-64 and T-72. By the early 1960s the Bundeswehr was already looking to develop a new generation of MBTs to match their Soviet adversaries.

(below) A Bundeswehr Leopard 1A5 takes up position during a Field Training Exercise. The Bundeswehr Leopard 1 tank battalions were crewed largely by conscripts and extensively planned defensive tactics during the Cold War, even extending to previously surveyed fire positions. (Jurgen Scholz)

THE DEVELOPMENT OF THE LEOPARD 2

In August 1963 the FDR and the United States of America signed a bilateral agreement to develop a new MBT to replace the M48. This new tank, the MBT70/ Kampfpanzer 70, was to be a revolutionary design. It would feature hydropneumatic suspension, the ability to fire on the move using a fully stabilised and tracked main gun, and an automatic loader. Moreover, its primary armament was to be the US 152mm Shillelagh combination weapon capable of firing conventional rounds and the guided missiles. The first prototype was to be delivered by March 1967. Although prototypes were built in each country, no agreement could be reached over key decisions, such as the power pack and the suspension and in 1969, with a cost of some 30million DM, the project was terminated.

Unable under the terms of the bilateral agreement to develop an MBT with other nations, the Germans had meanwhile begin a separate project, ostensibly to test technical components and extend the service life of the Leopard 1. In 1970 two prototypes, the so-called 'Vergoldeter'(Gilded) Leopard', were were handed over to the Bundeswehr. These had been assembled by Krauss-Maffei in Munich, with Porsche in Stuttgart also involved in the development of the hull and Wegmann in Kassel in that of the turret. In the same year, with the end of the MBT 70 project, the German government decided to press ahead with the development of a completely new MBT using lessons learned and technology gained from the bilateral project. In 1971 it was decided to abandon

the missile-firing capability of the MBT 70, but to keep its engine. Thus the engine compartment of the new tank had to be large enough to accommodate the Daimler-Benz MB 873 Ka-500 ten-cylinder engine developed for the MBT-70.

Beginning in 1970 Krauss-Maffei began the assembly of seventeen prototype turrets, ten armed with a 105mm smoothbore gun and the remainder with a 120mm smoothbore cannon, both developed by Rheinmetall. Sixteen of the planned seventeen chassis were built, fourteen with a conventional torsion bar suspension and the other two with the innovative hydropneumatic system developed for the MBT 70. These prototypes very much resembled the Leopard 1 with a sloping turret, but had a completely new hull while using the tracks and roadwheels from the MBT-70. By 1973 the first prototypes were ready for testing by the Bundeswehr and two years later two vehicles were shipped to Canada and the United States for testing under climatic extremes.

These prototypes had already exceeded the specified 50-ton weight limit, so Wegmann developed a lighter turret known as the 'Spitzmaus-Turm' (Shrew Turret). This was also fitted with the state-of the-art EMES 13 co-relation rangefinder than could be incorporated in the turret front. This was included in subsequent prototype turrets. The experience of Israeli armour during the 1973 Yom Kippur War had reinforced the primacy of armour in the minds of Western tank designers and, in October 1974, it was accepted that the new German tank would

This is one of the first Leopard 2 prototypes. It currently resides at the Bundeswehr Technical Centre for Land-Based Vehicle Systems, Engineer and General Field Equipment (WTD 41) in Trier. It combines chassis PT15 and turret T02. It is armed with the 105mm gun and outwardly resembles the Leopard 1 in appearance. (Sonaz)

have to have an increased maximum weight of 60 tons. One of the existing prototype turrets was thus modified with a new type of multi-layered armour.

On 11 December 1974 the FDR and the United States signed a Memorandum of Agreement to standardise certain components of their new Main Battle Tanks. This included joint trials of the putative Leopard 2 and the American prototype, Chrysler's XM1. As a result Krauss-Maffei assembled two new prototype chassis and three turrets. This version was known as the Leopard 2 AV ('Austere Version'). This tank was the first to have the characteristic slab-sided turret of the production-series Leopard 2. Each of the turrets had different configurations of sights and gunner's controls. Two were initially fitted with the 105mm gun for testing in the United States, while the third prototype turret was fitted with the 120mm gun from the outset. In August 1976 one complete prototype Leopard 2AV, one hull with extra weight to simulate the weight of the turret, and a separate hull and turret were flown to the United States for trials.

The trials were held at the Aberdeen Proving Ground in Maryland between September and December 1976. The XM1 had previously undergone the same test regime. The Leopard 2AV was found to be the equal of the XM1 in terms of both firepower and mobility, but the German tank had superior protection. It was with some degree of chagrin that the German designers realised that many of the innovations in the two

prototypes sent to America three years earlier had shaped the development of the XM1. For political reasons as much as military and technological, at the end of the trials the two nations decided to press ahead with the development of their own MBTs, the 105mm-armed M1 Abrams and the 120mm-armed Leopard 2. In 1977 the decision to procure the Leopard 2 as the Bundeswehr's new Main Battle Tank was approved by the FDR's Board of Defence and Budget Committee. 1,800 Leopard 2s were to be built and delivered to the Bundeswehr in five production batches. Two companies, Krauss-Maffei and Maschinenbau GmbH of Kiel (MaK) were selected as the main contractors for series production, with Krauss-Maffei producing 55% of the new tanks and MaK the remainder. Waggonfabrik und Fahrzeugbau Wegmann of Kassel was given responsibility for the turrets and the EMES 15 fire control system. It was decided to expedite the delivery of the new tank to the Bundeswehr even though some components, most notably the planned thermal tank sights, were not yet ready. In October 1978 Krauss-Maffei handed over the first completed chassis to the Bundeswehr for approval and in the following February two more production-series vehicles and a third turret were completed for testing at the German Armour School in Münster. These proved successful and on 25 October 1979 in a ceremony at the German Armour School the Bundeswehr received its first Leopard 2 into service.

(top) Prototype turret T11 was fitted with a 20mm remotely operated autocannon, one of the original concepts for the MBT 70. The other prototype turrets were fitted with a machine gun.

(right) Leopard 2AV prototype PT19 fitted with the 120mm Rheinmetall main gun-armed T21 turret.

LEOPARD 2A0 TO 2A3

After the first Leopard 2 was handed over to the German Armour School in October 1979 serial production got underway at Krauss-Maffei and MaK. A total of 380 were built in the first series, the first tanks replacing the M48A5G in 1 and 3 Panzerdivisionen of I (GE) Corps. By 1980 the Leopard 2A0 was also replacing the M48A2G in the Panzergrenadier divisions. Some changes were introduced during this first production run, most notably reinforcing the cooling air outlet grille with vertical bars from the 28th vehicle. Second series production commenced in March 1982 and by November the following year a further 248 tanks had been built by Krauss-Maffei and 202 by MaK. A number of changes were introduced: the crosswind sensor was deleted, a tank thermal sight was introduced, the fuel fillers on the engine deck were repositioned and longer tow cables, now crossed at the rear, were introduced. These second series vehicles were known as Leopard 2A1, as were the third series vehicles (165 by Krauss Maffei and 135 by MaK) built between November 1983 and November 1983. This batch also featured a shot deflector to the redesigned commander's Peri R-17 panoramic sight, as

well as the modified engine grillee. Between 1984 and 1987 first series vehicles were returned to the factory to be rebuilt to the latest standard and repainted in the new three-colour NATO scheme. These vehicles were known as Leopard 2A2.

Between December 1984 and December 1985 Krauss-Maffei built 165 and Mak 135 tanks of the fourth series. Externally these vehicles were identifiable by the shorter antennae of the SEM 80/90 VHF radios and the fact that they left the factory sporting the three-colour NATO camouflage scheme. Moreover, the ammunition supply hatch on the left-hand side of the turret was welded shut as tests had revealed that, if hit, it would compromise the tank's NBC protection. These tanks were designated Leopard 2A3.

The introduction of the Leopard 2 into the Bundeswehr was not without its teething problems. The tank was vastly superior to both the Leopard 1 and M48, but required very different tactics to those previously employed (which differed very little from World War II Panzer tactics). Problems with the availability of spare parts, inadequate training, and wear and tear meant that many Leopard 2 units in the early and mid 1980s operated at less than 50% readiness.

A Leopard 2A1 of Panzerbataillon 23 lurks in cover during Exercise Bellende Meute ('Barking Pack') that took place in Lower Saxony in September 1983. Panzerbataillon 23 received its complement of Leopard 2s between November 1981 and October the following year. (Eckhard Ude)

A fifth-series Leopard 2A4 from 20 (GE) Panzerbrigade, operating alongside 3 (UK) Armoured Division during Exercise Iron Hammer in November 1988. (Eckhard Ude)

LEOPARD 2A4

The Leopard 2A4 was the standard version of the Leopard 2 that equipped the Bundeswehr and served with many other NATO nations from the mid 1980s to the present day. Production of the Leopard 2A4 began at Krauss-Maffei and MaK in December 1985 with the fifth-series production batch. 190 fifth-series tanks were built at Krauss-Maffei and 180 at Mak up to March 1987. The main changes to this batch from previous tanks included a digital upgrade to the fire control computer (the DigBal or Digital Ballistic Processing Unit) and the installation of an internal fire suppression system. A central warning light was also fitted in front of the driver's position. Newly built vehicles were also fitted with the SEM 80/90 radio (while upgraded tanks could retain the older SEM 23/35 radio and did so until the mid 1990s). Towards the end of the production run the second and third return rollers were also repositioned. The very last Krauss-Maffei-built vehicles also had the ammunition supply hatch on the left-hand side of the turret deleted.

The fifth series was intended to the final production batch of the Leopard 2, but in June 1987 a further order for 83 Krauss-Maffei and 67 MaK tanks was placed. These were completed between January 1988 and May 1989. Most notably these tanks left the factory in the new zinc-chromate-based standard three-colour NATO camouflage, although from the mid 1980s older tanks had been repainted in this scheme. These tanks also received the new heavier front sections of the side skirts from the 97th vehicle in the production run, as well as the new Diehl 570FT tracks. The ammunition supply hatch was deleted from all tanks in this production batch. In May 1989 production of the seventh-series began, ending in April 1990 with 55 built by Krauss-Maffei and 45 by MaK. The tanks in this production batch were identical to those of the sixth-series.

Between January 1991 and March 1992 an additional 75 vehicles (41 by Krauss-Maffei and 34 by MaK) were built as the eighth-series production batch. The distinctive feature of this batch, introduced soon after production had commenced, was a new six part rear side skirt. The vehicles in this batch also received reinforced launchers in the bottom row of the turret smoke-grenade system. Later tanks were also fitted with a collimator on the right side of the mouth of the 120mm main gun as part of the muzzle reference system. The final Leopard 2A4 was accepted into the Bundeswehr's

Photographed during the same exercise, this fifth-series Leopard 2A4 has prominent Orange Forces crosses applied over the national markings and on the front of the turret. (Eckhard Ude)

Another fifth-series Leopard 2A4 (note the welded shut ammunition resupply hatch below the national marking) from Aufklärungs Bataillon 7 on Exercise Golden Knight in June 2000. Note also how the barrel cleaning rods, usually fitted on the glacis plate, are attached to the turret side. (Eckhard Ude)

Gebirgs-Panzerbataillon 8 in March 1992. Earlier Leopard 2s were rebuilt periodically, with older hulls being mated with newer turrets. All tanks fitted with the DigBal system were known as Leopard 2A4 in Bundeswehr service regardless of any other external fixtures.

Originally the German government had procured 1,800 Leopard 2 for the Bundeswehr, but by March 1992 a total of 2,215 tanks had been produced for German use. In addition 445 tanks had been built for the Netherlands and 380 for Switzerland.

From 1994, as we shall see, the Germans begin selling off surplus stocks of Leopard 2A4s. Initially, these were from the first to fourth production series, Leopard 2A0 to Leopard 2A3, which had been upgraded to Leopard 2A4 standard. By 2007 the Germans had sold 1,459 Leopard 2A4 to foreign users, mostly NATO members but also including Chile (172 tanks) and Singapore (182 tanks). Similarly, the Dutch sold off most of their stocks of Leopard 2A4 between 1998 (114 sold to Austria) and 2008 (80 tanks to Canada).

A nice front-on image of a Leopard 2A4 of the same unit, also photographed during Exercise Golden Knight. The photograph affords a good view of the warning light fitted in front of the driver's station. (Eckhard Ude)

LEOPARD 2A5

The imperative to modernise NATO's tank forces to meet the new generation of Soviet MBTs, principally the T-80, had continued throughout the 1970s into the next decade. However, in 1982 plans to develop a joint Franco-German MBT collapsed and the modernisation of the existing Leopard 2 fleet were first seriously considered in 1984. The so-called Peace Dividend, a reduction in defence expenditure by NATO governments as a result of the collapse of the Soviet Union, put pay to many defence programmes across NATO (including the putative Leopard 3), but Germany, the Netherlands and Switzerland decided to continue with plans to modify 699 Leopard 2A4 of the sixth to eighth series under the *Kampfwertsteigerungen* or KWS (Combat Capability Improvement Programme). The original plan for the KWS envisaged three levels: KWS I, the replacement of the 120mm L/44 gun with an L/55 cannon and the introduction of new kinetic energy ammunition; KWS II, improved armour protection and command and control (C2) systems; KWS III, a 140mm main gun in a new turret (development stopped in 1995).

In fact, it was the KWS Level II improvements that were the first to be implemented. A test-bed prototype chassis was chosen (a fifth-series Leopard 2A4) in 1989 to implement the proposed armour improvements. The weight limit for the new package was set at 62.5 tonnes. The new armour mounted on the turret front and chassis radically altered the appearance of the Leopard 2; the characteristic box-like turret of the Leopard 2A0 to 2A4 disappeared under angular add-on modules. This initial test-bed also featured an electric gun control system, internal turret spall liners, armoured roadwheel hubs, a driver's sliding hatch and modified commander's periscopes. The turret armour modules necessitated the relocation of the EMES 15A2 viewfinder to the turret roof in a new armoured housing and the commander's Peri R17 was enhanced with a second-generation thermal sight and relocated to the left rear

(above) Leopard 2A5NL serving as part of SFOR, NATO's peace-keeping force in Bosnia-Herzegovina, during Operation Joint Guard. The additional turret armour radically alters the appearance of the tank. (Peter van Iren)

(below A good head-on view of a Leopard 2A5NL in Bosnia showing the relocated EMES 15A2 gun sight in its armoured housing. (Peter van Iren)

of the commander's cupola. Two further eighth-series Leopard 2A4 were also fitted with slightly different packages as part of the KWS II evaluation process.

In March 1992 representatives of Germany, the Netherlands and Switzerland met in Mannheim to agree the final configuration of the modified Leopard 2. The 'Mannheim Configuration' featured the new commander's periscope (the Peri R17A2) with thermal sight and laser rangefinder, electric gun control system to replace the hydraulic system on previous Leopard 2s, and the new external and internal turret armour. This latter modification necessitated raising the height of the EMES 15A2. The sliding driver's hatch, uparmoured roadwheels with steel instead of aluminium hubs, new stowage baskets on the turret rear, and a rear-view camera were also agreed upon. The older-pattern side skirts were also replaced with newly designed ones. As well as these external changes, a host of internal improvements were introduced: these included improvements to the EMES 15A2 main gun sight, an electronic firing system which reduced the delay between the gunner pulling the trigger and the shot being fired, and enhancements to the range of the fire control system. The additional armour packages for the turret roof and hull front, as well as a spall liner for the hull, were not adopted, presumably due to cost constraints. Another test-bed chassis was made up with these modifications and extensively tested between November 1993 and September the following year. The KWS I improvements were put on hold for the time being and the go ahead was given to convert the first batch of 225 Leopard 2A4 (mostly from the sixth to eighth series) to Leopard 2A5 standard. A small number of tanks were upgraded to Leopard 2A5A1 command vehicles through the installation of the SEM 93 VHF radio. The Netherlands approved the conversion of 330 vehicles, with the first Leopard 2A5NLs being delivered to 42 Tankbataljon in May 1997, while the Swiss agreed to follow suit at an unspecified future date.

The first Leopard 2A5 were delivered to the German Armoured Forces School in November 1995 and the first combat unit (Panzerbataillon 33) received the new tank a month or so later. These first Leopard 2A5s were distributed across six armoured battalions. A second batch of conversions saw a planned further 125 vehicles converted to Leopard 2A5. In all, however, only 285 tanks were modified to Leopard 2A5 as the final 65 vehicles also received the KWS I modification converting them to Leopard 2A6 standard. The Leopard 2A5 continued to serve alongside the Leopard 2A6 in the Bundeswehr even after the conclusion of the KWS Level 1 programme. In 1996 Dutch Leopard 2A5s were deployed to Bosnia as part of Operation Joint Guard, while three years later 28 Leopard 2A5 of Panzerbataillonen 33 and 214 were deployed to Kosovo as part of the NATO mission there. In 2013 the Bundeswehr agreed to sell 105 of its 125 Leopard 2A5 to Poland and most of the remaining vehicles (seventeen tanks) remain in service as OPFOR vehicles at the German Army Combat Training Centre at Letzlingen.

Leopard 2A5 at the German Armour School in 2010. (Bundeswehr)

LEOPARD 2A6

The KWS Level I improvements were designed to increase the firepower of the 120mm main, allowing it to penetrate the latest third-generation MBT armour, while retaining the current calibre and fire-control systems. The barrel length was extended by 11 calibres (1320mm) and a new generation of kinetic energy ammunition, including a longer tungsten penetrator for the APFSDS (Armour-Piercing, Fin-Stabilised Discarding Sabot) round was introduced. A tungsten penetrator was preferred over the depleted-uranium penetrators used by the US and Britain for political reasons. Rheinmetall also developed a new propellant that enabled these new rounds to be fired from the older L/44 barrel, so it was not until 1997 that the KWS Level I improvements were tested on two modified Leopard 2A5 from Panzerbataillon 33.

In 2001 the final 65 Leopard 2A4 due to be upgraded to 2A5 standard were also fitted with the new L/55 main gun. On 7 March the first Leopard 2A6, as these tanks were known, was delivered to Panzerbataillon 403. Initially all German Leopard 2A5 were intended to be converted to 2A6, but this programme was terminated before the second batch had been completed and, as a resut, 125 Leopard 2A5 remained in Bundeswehr service. Apart from the L/55 gun, there are no other external differences between the Leopard 2A5 and the 2A6 in Bundeswehr service.

With the end of the Cold War a new set of priorities emerged in MBT protection. Deployment on NATO missions to the Balkans revealed the vulnerability of MBTs to IEDs (Improvised Explosive Devices) and mines. In 2001 ballistic tests revealed weaknesses in the belly armour of the Leopard 2 and Germany, the Netherlands, Sweden and Switzerland cooperated in a programme to improve the mine protection of the Leopard 2A6. In 2004 the Bundeswehr procured fifteen tanks with additional belly armour to protect against mines and IEDs. Improvements to crew protection were also made in the hull and turret interior. These tanks were known as Leopard 2A6M. These were delivered in 2004-5, with an additional 55 tanks modified in 2006-7. Of these seventy tanks, 48 remain in active service with the Bundeswehr (with two as reference vehicles), the remainder being handed over to the Canadians in 2007 for their deployment to Afghanistan. By 2008 the Bundeswehr had 350 Leopard 2A5, 2A6 and 2A6M in active service.

The Leopard 2A6 was intended to equip all the armoured battalions of the Bundeswehr's Crisis Intervention Force, but under the 'Heer 2011' reorganisation the number of armoured battalions was reduced by two to five and the tank force reduced from its Cold War height of 2,125 to just 225 vehicles (seventeen Leopard 2A5, 141 Leopard 2A6, 48 Leopard 2A6M, nineteen Leopard 2A7). However, the Russian annexation of Crimea and war in the Donbass in 2014 forced a reconsideration of the importance of the MBT in NATO armies. Consequently, a decision was taken to activate a sixth armoured battalion and upgrade all Bundeswehr tanks to Leopard 2A7 or 2A7V standard. The cost of upgrading the entire tank fleet in one

The typical appearance of the Leopard 2A6 in Bundeswehr service. This tank of Panzerlehrbataillon 93 is camouflaged with hessian, camouflage netting and foliage. It is also fitted with the rubber skirts on the hull and turret front designed to reduce the tank's thermal signature. (Ralph Zwilling)

A Leopard 2A6M of Panzerbataillon 393 at the German Army Combat Training Centre during Exercise White Rose in January 2016. (Ralph Zwilling)

go was prohibitive, however, so from 2015 through to the end of 2017 fifty Leopard 2A6M received some of the 2A7 upgrades at the Krauss-Maffei plant in Munich as an interim measure. This version is known as Leopard 2A6M+. These modifications included principally a turret stowage box for the crew's small arms and the new ATTICA third-generation thermal sight for the commander's panoramic periscope (designated Peri R17A3), and a new SOTAS-IP intercommunication system with infantry phone. From 2018 the fifty Leopard 2A6M+ were also fitted with the new *Integriertes Führungs- und Informationssystem* (IFIS) command and control system software that allows digital integration at battalion level across all the Bundeswehr's troops and combat vehicles.

A Leopard 2A6M of Panzerbataillon 393 takes part in Exercise Iron Wolf 2018 in Lithuania as part of NATO Enhanced Forward Presence in the Baltic States and Poland. (Stefan Degraef)

Leopard 2A6 of Panzerlehrbataillon 93, assigned to NATO's Very High Readiness Joint Task Force (VJTF), take part in Exercise Noble Jump in June 2019. (US Army photo by SFC Michael O'Brien)

LEOPARD 2A7

The latest variant of the Leopard 2 to enter Bundeswehr service has done so via a somewhat circuitous route. In 2006, in response to the new threat that MBTs faced in asymmetrical conflicts such as those in Balkans or Iraq, Krauss-Maffei Wegmann (KMW), unveiled its Leopard 2 PSO (Peace Support Operations). Based upon a modified Leopard 2A6NL, it could fire new HE (High Explosive) ammunition, had the IFIS C2 system installed, as well as an APU (auxiliary power unit) allowing the tanks electrical systems to run without the main engine being on, a new crew compartment heating system, a dozer blade, a FLT RWS (Remote Weapons System), a commander's Peri-RTWL panoramic periscope, the SPECTUS driver's day and night sight system, an infantry communications system, all-round CCTV facility, mine protection as fitted to the Leopard 2A6M,

A Leopard 2A7 of Panzerbataillon 203. On the side skirts you can discern the velcro mounting points for Saab's thermal protection system, the Barracuda Mobile Camouflage System. This had first been used on Canadian and Danish Leopard 2s deployed to Afghanistan. (Ralph Zwilling)

and frontal armour the same as the Leopard 2E. It was also fitted with slat armour to protect from rocket-propelled grenades. Originally 150 Leopard 2A6M were to be converted to the PSO standard, but financial constraints saw this abandoned in favour of projects like the GTK Boxer and Puma IFV (Infantry Fighting Vehicle). KMW added further enhancements to the vehicle and in 2010 exhibited it as the Leopard 2A7+. 62 of these vehicles were subsequently ordered by Qatar in 2013 and in December 2018 Hungary announced its intention to purchase this version of the Leopard 2.

As we will see, in 2007 Canada received twenty German Leopard 2A6Ms for deployment to Afghanistan. Instead of returning these tanks as planned at the end of the lease, the Canadians purchased surplus Leopard 2A6NL, converted them to 2A6M standard and returned these tanks to Germany. They were then modified at the KMW plant for return to the Bundeswehr. KMW used this opportunity to introduce a range of upgrades previously planned for the Leopard 2 PSO. These included the APU, capacity to fire the new HE ammunition, the IFIS C2 system, the infantry intercom system, a new fire suppression system, the new Peri R7A3 (as fitted to the Leopard 2A6M+), and preparation for add-on armour. The RWS was not installed, nor were the 360 degree CCTV and other features that would have optimised the tank for urban or asymmetrical warfare. The Leopard 2A7, as this variant is known, is designed for a peer or near-peer adversary. The first

vehicles were delivered in December 2014 and currently Panzerbataillon 203 fields fourteen of these tanks.

The situation in Ukraine prompted a re-evaluation of the role of the MBT in NATO armies. Consequently, the Bundeswehr decided to activate a sixth tank battalion and return 104 Leopard 2A6NLs and 2A4s currently in stowage to service. These tanks are being upgraded at KMW to Leopard 2A7V (Verbessert or 'improved') standard. This is a much more substantial modification than that to 2A7 standard and involves a new L55A1 main gun capable of firing the DM11 programmable HE round. This gun can also fire a new APFSDS round. The Leopard 2A7V also has the enhanced frontal armour seen on the most modern Swedish, Danish and Greek Leopard 2s. The APU, NBC and air conditioning systems are all enhanced, as are the crew optics and the tank's ability to operate alongside other NATO forces on the digital battlefield. The Bundeswehr will receive its full complement of Leopard 2A7V by 2023, while Denmark is similarly upgrading its fleet of Leopard 2A5DK. Hungary also confirmed its order and will receive 44 Leopard 2A7V. On 29 October 2019 KMW handed over the first German and first Danish Leopard 2A7s to their respective new owners, almost exactly four decades after the Leopard 2 had first entered service with the Bundeswehr. With this upgrade the Leopard 2 has retained its claim to be the most powerful MBT in NATO's arsenal and quite possibly 'the world's best tank'.

A good shot of the Leopard 2A7 crew in action. Note the commander is using the portable display for the Rocky RK9 notebook part of the Integriertes Führungs- und Informationssystem (IFIS). IFIS is currently fitted to the Leopard 2A7, GTK Boxer and Puma IVF. These crew members are also wearing the new Bose-manufactured tank helmet. (Ralph Zwilling)

LEOPARD 2 IN FOREIGN SERVICE
AUSTRIA

In 1998 Austria purchased 114 surplus Leopard 2NLs, built to A4 standard, from the Netherlands. The Austrians had previously used the US M60 MBT and in the late 1980s had received the latest M60A3 as these were phased out in the US Army with the introduction of the M1A1 Abrams. The new tanks were designated Leopard 2A4Ö (for Österreich) and the last vehicle was received in October 2000. Originally, the Leopard 2A4Ö operated in its original Dutch configuration, but in 2003 they received the German digitised smoke dischargers (although this was not universal throughout the entire fleet) VIC3 Intercom and radios, and the fighting compartment fire suppression system. They retained, however, the American style antennae. The Austrian Bundesheer currently fields 56 tanks in a single tank battalion. The Austrian Leopard units are well trained and in 2017 crews operating the Leopard 2A4Ö won the Strong Europe Tank Challenge, seeing off rivals crews from France (Leclerc 2), Germany (Leopard 2A6M), Poland (Leopard 2A5), Ukraine (T-64BM) and the United States (M1A2 SEPV2).

A Leopard 2A4Ö of Panzerbataillon 33: note the smoke dischargers, the same as those fitted to the German Leopard 2A6, and the FN MAG machine gun on the loader's cupola. (R888)

Leopard 2A4Ö, a tank of the winning team of the Strong Europe Tank Challenge at the Grafenwöhr Training Area, Germany, in May 2017. (US Army photo by Spc. Nathanael Mercado)

A Leopard 2A6M CAN of Lord Strathcona's Horse (Royal Canadians) takes up position in Kandahar Province, Afghanistan. (Canadian Combat Camera/Anthony Sewards)

CANADA

Canada is one of the most important users of the Leopard 2 and one of only four NATO members to have deployed the tank in a combat situation. In 1988 Canada had trialled the Leopard 2 as a possible successor to the Leopard 1, but these plans were cancelled with the end of the Cold War. The Canadian government finally took the decision to procure the Leopard 2 in 2006 amidst unusual circumstances. From 2000 Canada was phasing its fleet of Leopard 1 MBTs out of service and considering replacing them with the Stryker Mobile Gun System, a 105mm tank gun mounted on a derivative of the LAV III 8x8 wheeled vehicle, already in service with the Canadian army. The Canadian deployment to Afghanistan and their take-over as lead nation of the ISAF (International Security Assistance Force) in Kandahar Province in August 2003 changed all that. In 2006 the Canadians launched a major offensive against the Taliban, Operation Medusa, and it became clear that the LAV III was

not sufficient to dislodge a well dug-in and determined enemy. The Leopard 1 fleet, in the process of being sold, scrapped or put in museums, was brought out of mothballs and 66 of the original 114 tanks made ready for service and possible deployment to Afghanistan. It soon became apparent that the Leopard C2, a modernised Leopard 1A5 with new Modular Expandable Armour System (MEXAS), deployed from December 2006 was not sufficient for the Canadian army's urgent operational requirement. A new tank was needed with increased firepower and protection and an air-conditioning facility to combat the searing temperatures encountered in Afghanistan.

In Feburary 2007 initial enquiries were made to procure Leopard 2s from Germany. Only the Bundeswehr's Leopard 2A6M, with its additional belly armour, provided the necessary defence against mines and IEDs and in April that year the Germans agreed to loan twenty tanks and two Armoured

....*text continued on page 46*

A good rear view of a Leopard 2A6M CAN in its current configuration. Note the modified rear turret stowage, the Canadian antenna and the turret roof stowage. (Matthew Worth)

COLOUR PROFILES BY
SLAWOMIR ZAJACZKOWSKI

(left) A Leopard 2NL of C Squadron, 41st Tank Tankbataljon, moves through a West German village during Exercise Free Lion 88. (*NIHM Collectie Nederlands Instituut voor Militaire Historie*)

1. Leopard 2NL, 41st Tank Tankbataljon, Exercise Free Lion, Germany, September 1988.

Between 19-23 September 1988 the 1st (NL) Corps conducted its last corps-level field training exercise (FTX) of the Cold War. Some 44,000 troops took part, including British, West German and American soldiers, alongside their Dutch allies. No fewer than 420 MBTs took part, including the Leopard 2NLs of 41st Tank Battalion, one of three battalions so equipped in the Koninklijke Landmacht. The tank is painted in the distinctive 'Army Green' used by the Koninklijke Landmacht before the adoption of the three-colour NATO scheme in the early 1990s.

2

2. Panzer 87, Switzerland, mid 1990s.
This is one of the last production Panzer 87, a tank basically identical to the fifth and sixth-series production Leopard 2A4. Note the track grousers attached to the front of the turret and the special exhaust muffler, designed to suppress the sound of the exhaust in the heavily populated Swiss cantons. The tank is painted in a distinctive version of the standard three-colour NATO scheme.

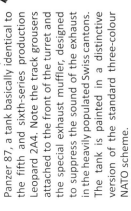

(right) A Panzer 87 WE of Mechanised Brigade 11 moves at speed across the training area. *(Photo: Swiss Army)*

3. Leopard 2A4FIN, Finnish Armoured Brigade, Finland, 2003. This is one of the first of 124 Leopard 2A4s the Finns received from Germany in 2003. Note the distinctive double handrail added to the front of the turret, enlarged turret rear and modified rear side skirt. The Finns are unusual in that their tanks sport national roundels, in blue and white. The splinter camouflage, introduced in 1981, consists of two shades of green - Vaaleanvihreä (AN22) and Tummanvihreä (AN11) –and NATO Black.

(right) A Finnish Leopard 2A6 in 2016 showing clearly the distinctive three-colour splinter camouflage.

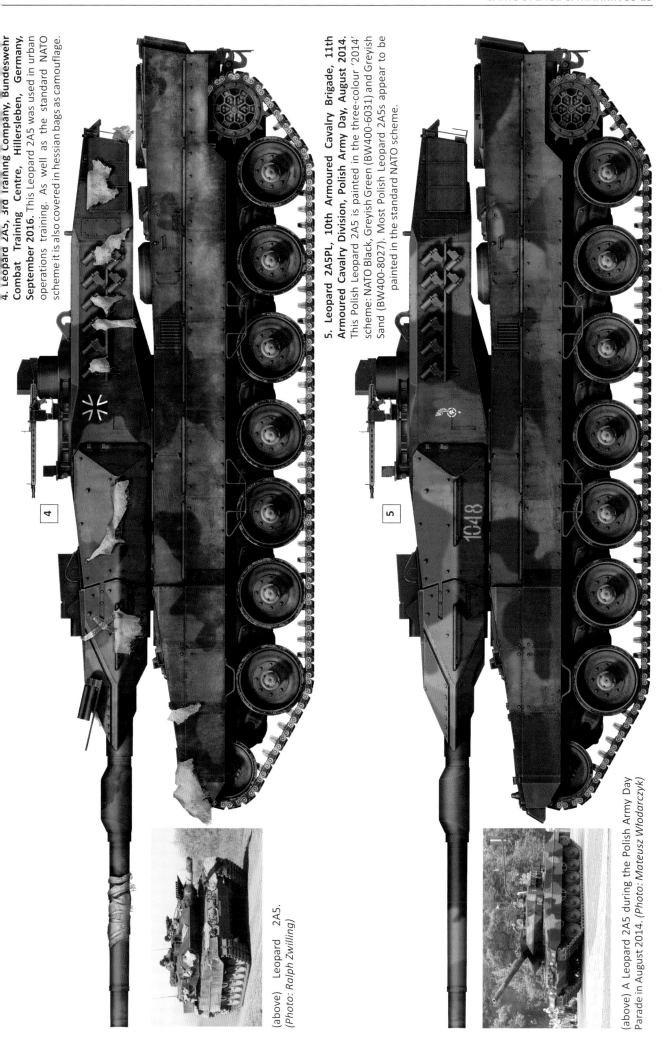

4. Leopard 2A5, 3rd Training Company, Bundeswehr Combat Training Centre, Hillersleben, Germany, September 2016. This Leopard 2A5 was used in urban operations training. As well as the standard NATO scheme it is also covered in hessian bags as camouflage.

5. Leopard 2A5PL, 10th Armoured Cavalry Brigade, 11th Armoured Cavalry Division, Polish Army Day, August 2014. This Polish Leopard 2A5 is painted in the three-colour '2014' scheme: NATO Black, Greyish Green (BW400-6031) and Greyish Sand (BW400-8027). Most Polish Leopard 2A5s appear to be painted in the standard NATO scheme.

(above) Leopard 2A5. (*Photo: Ralph Zwilling*)

(above) A Leopard 2A5 during the Polish Army Day Parade in August 2014. (*Photo: Mateusz Włodarczyk*)

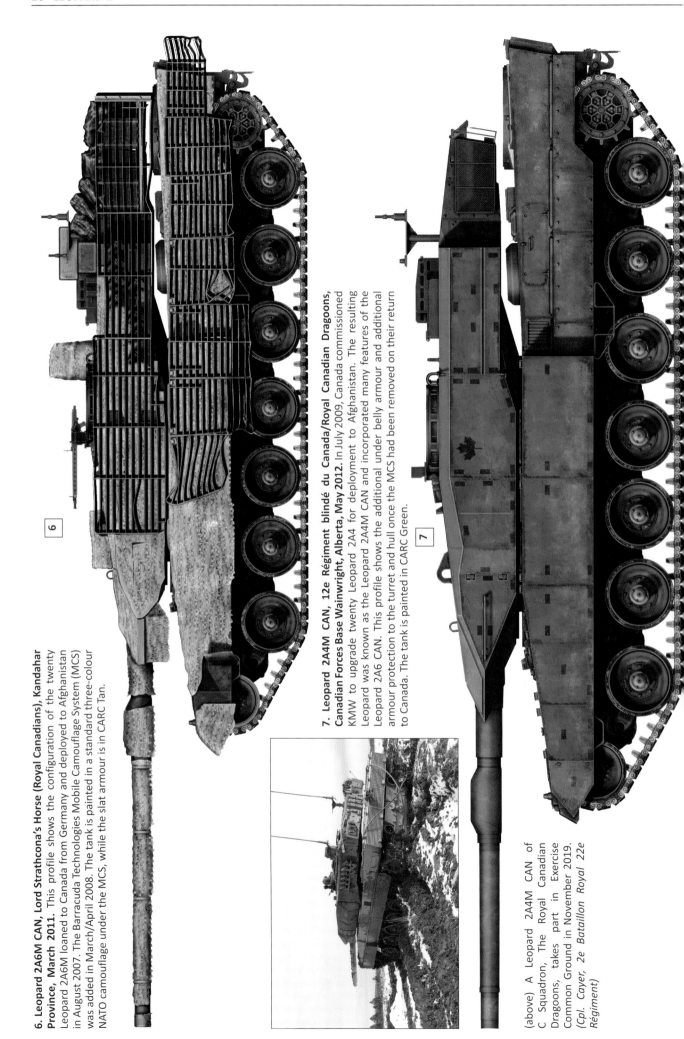

6. Leopard 2A6M CAN, Lord Strathcona's Horse (Royal Canadians), Kandahar Province, March 2011. This profile shows the configuration of the twenty Leopard 2A6M loaned to Canada from Germany and deployed to Afghanistan in August 2007. The Barracuda Technologies Mobile Camouflage System (MCS) was added in March/April 2008. The tank is painted in a standard three-colour NATO camouflage under the MCS, while the slat armour is in CARC Tan.

7. Leopard 2A4M CAN, 12e Régiment blindé du Canada/Royal Canadian Dragoons, Canadian Forces Base Wainwright, Alberta, May 2012. In July 2009, Canada commissioned KMW to upgrade twenty Leopard 2A4 for deployment to Afghanistan. The resulting Leopard was known as the Leopard 2A4M CAN and incorporated many features of the Leopard 2A6 CAN. This profile shows the additional under belly armour and additional armour protection to the turret and hull once the MCS had been removed on their return to Canada. The tank is painted in CARC Green.

(above) A Leopard 2A4M CAN of C Squadron, The Royal Canadian Dragoons, takes part in Exercise Common Ground in November 2019. (*Cpl. Cayer, 2e Bataillon Royal 22e Régiment*)

8. Leopard 2A5DK, Jutland Dragoon Regiment, Nordic Tank Challenge, Holstebro, Denmark, May 2016. The Nordic Tank Challenge was one of a series of events that pitted NATO crews and their vehicles in tests of gunnery and other skills. Two tanks crews each from Sweden, Norway, Canada, Germany, Poland, Denmark and the United States. The Danish crews in their Leopard 2A5DK from 2nd Tank Squadron, Jutland Dragoon Regiment, won the event on their home turf.

(right) Leopard 2A5DKs of the Jutland Dragoon Regiment at the Nordic Tank Challenge in May 2016. *(US Army photo by Staff Sgt. Michael Behlin)*

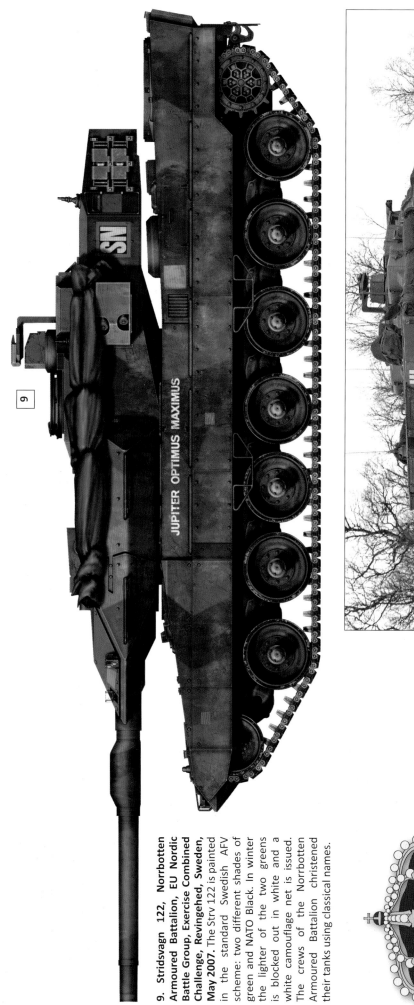

9 |

9. Stridsvagn 122, Norrbotten Armoured Battalion, EU Nordic Battle Group, Exercise Combined Challenge, Revingehed, Sweden, May 2007. The Strv 122 is painted in the standard Swedish AFV scheme: two different shades of green and NATO Black. In winter the lighter of the two greens is blocked out in white and a white camouflage net is issued. The crews of the Norrbotten Armoured Battalion christened their tanks using classical names.

(right) A Strv 122 of the tank company of the Skaraborg Regiment. *(Photo: Ralph Zwilling)*

10. Leopard 2A6NL, 11th Tankbataljon, Army Exhibition Day 2007, Wezep, Netherlands, June 2007. This tank was on display at the Dutch Army Exhibition Day in Wezep in Gelderland in June 2007. It is finished in the standard NATO scheme.

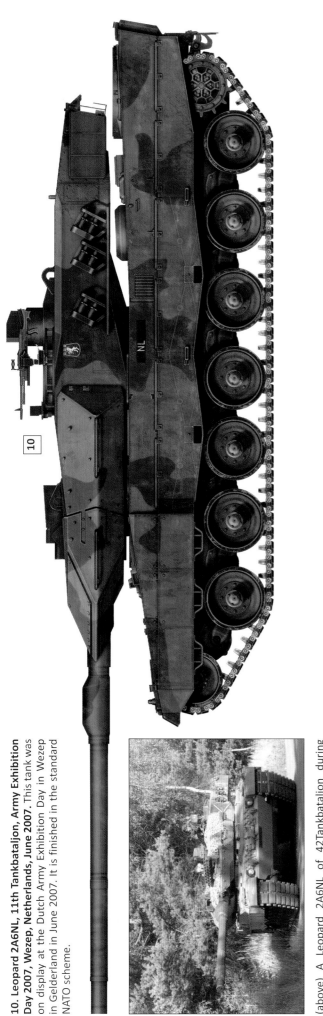

[10]

(above) A Leopard 2A6NL of 42Tankbataljon during Exercise Bison Prepare in Bergen Hohne, Germany in September 2004. *(NIHM Collectie Nederlands Instituut voor Militaire Historie)*

11. Leopard 2HEL, Hellenic Army, Oxi Day Parade, Thessaloniki, Greece, October 2018.

[11]

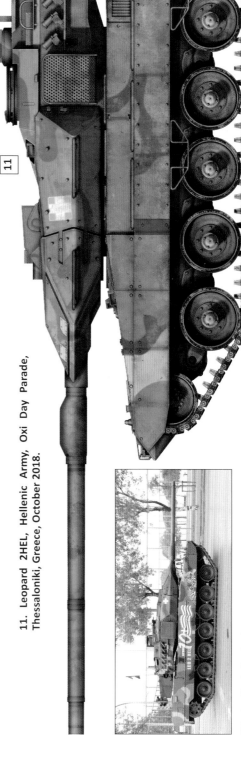

(Photo: Fanis Boskos)

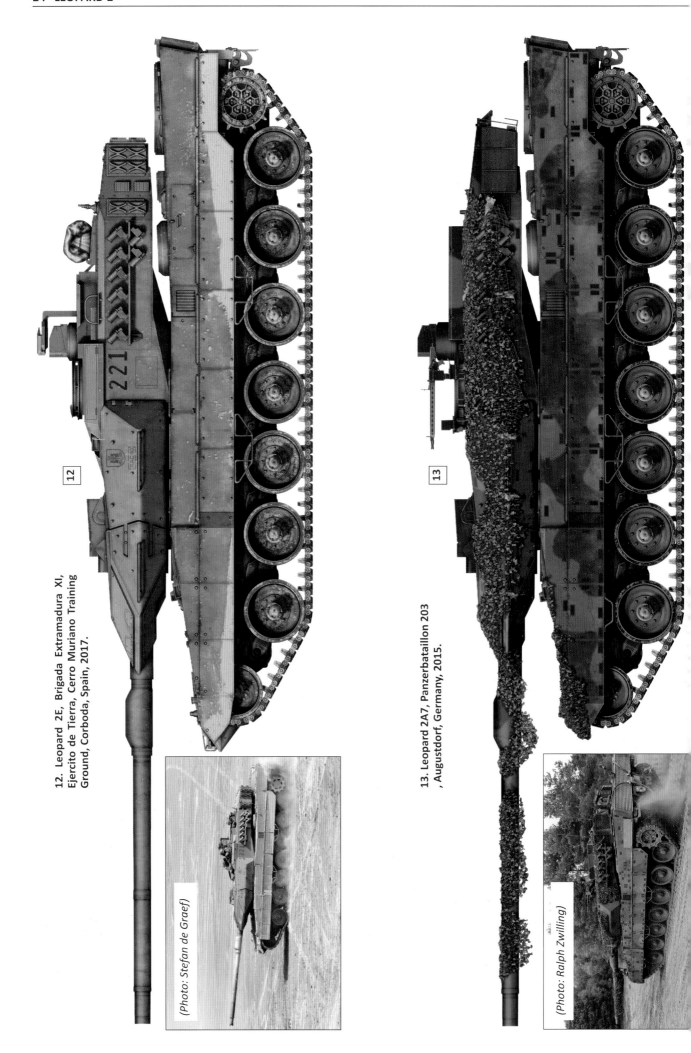

12. Leopard 2E, Brigada Extremadura XI, Ejercito de Tierra, Cerro Muriano Training Ground, Corboda, Spain, 2017.

(Photo: Stefan de Graef)

13. Leopard 2A7, Panzerbataillon 203, Augustdorf, Germany, 2015.

(Photo: Ralph Zwilling)

LEOPARD 2NL

41 TANKBATALJON, EXERCISE GRIFFIN ENFORCING, LOWER SAXONY, GERMANY, AUGUST 1997.

**1/35 SCALE
MENG MODEL
DAVID GRUMMITT**

(left Meng Model's Leopard 2A4 is the best kit of this version available and can be assembled out of the box into a Bundeswehr vehicle.

(right) Converting to Leopard 2NL requires either the Legend Productions' conversion kit (designed for the Leopard 2A5) or the parts from Revell's Leopard 2A5/A6NL kits. The model was further enhanced with Leopard Workshop's excellent American-style aerials and resin barrel.

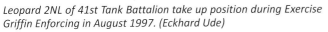

Leopard 2NL of 41st Tank Battalion take up position during Exercise Griffin Enforcing in August 1997. (Eckhard Ude)

Leopard 2NL cross the River Weser during the same Field Training Exercise. (Eckhard Ude)

LEOPARD 2A4FIN
HÄME ARMOURED BATTALION, FINNISH ARMY, 2015.
1/35 SCALE
MENG MODEL
IMAD BOUANTOUN

Meng Model's Leopard 2A4 is great kit and out of the box probably best represents a 5th series production Bundeswehr Leopard 2A4.

Here you can see some of the modifications made to represent a Leopard 2A4 FIN. These include the extra anti-slip texture to the turret roof, additional turret grab handles and the enlarged turret rear. The model was also detailed with Voyager's photoetch set.

(above) The additional stowage box on the left face of the turret is evident here.

(top right) Some good references were necessary to cut the sheet styrene for the turret rear. Note too the cut back side skirts.

(above right) Typical of Finnish Leopard 2s in the field: camouflage netting, white sheets and, of course, snow!

LEOPARD 2A5

3. KOMPANIE, PANZERBATAILLON 33, BUNDESWEHR, COMBAT MANUEVER TRAINING CENTER, HOHENFELS, APRIL 1997

1/35 SCALE TAMIYA
CHRIS JERRETT

Tamiya's Leopard 2A5 was upgraded with some scratchbuilt additions as well as resin parts from Perfect Scale Modellbau and the Eduard photoetched detail set.

A nice shot of the superdetailed engine deck. Note the additional turret weld seams that are missing from the Tamiya kit.

The vinyl tracks are the weakest part of the Tamiya kit so were replaced with the nicely detailed Bronco Models' tracks.

The three-tone NATO camouflage scheme was sprayed with Tamiya acrylics.

(below) A Leopard 2A5 of the Bundeswehr's Combat Training Centre in the Altmark. (Ralph Zwilling)

STRIDSVAGN 122

191ST MECHANISED BATTALION, NORBOTTEN REGIMENT, EXERCISE TRIDENT JUNCTURE 2017

1/35 SCALE HOBBYBOSS AND TAMIYA CHRIS JERRETT

(below) Hobbyboss's Strv 122 has a number of flaws, but you can combine it with Tamiya's excellent Leopard 2A5 for a more accurate model.

(right) Here you can see the white plasticard additions to the Hobbyboss turret.

(above) A good overall of the model before paint. Note the individual-link Bronco Models' tracks.

(below) Good references are the key when trying a 'kitbash' project like this.

(below) The distinctive splinter-pattern camouflage was applied using Tamiya acrylics and masking tape to get the hard-edged demarcations between colours.

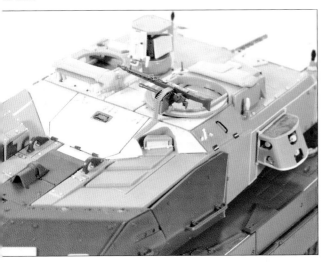

LEOPARD 2A6M CAN

LORD STRATHCONA'S HORSE (ROYAL CANADIANS), KANDAHAR PROVINCE, AFGHANISTAN, MAY 2008

1/35 SCALE TAMIYA/ HOBBYBOSS/ PERFECT SCALE MODELBAU, LESTER PLASKITT

The Perfect Scale Modelbau conversion transforms the base Hobbyboss kit, which itself was also improved by additions from Tamiya's Leopard 2A6.

The combination of plastic kit parts, photoetched details and scratchbuilt additions is evident from the superdetailed engine deck

The slat armour, carefully thinned down to a better scale representation, gives the Leopard 2A6M CAN a very different appearance to the Leopard 2A6 in European service.

Twenty Leopard 2A6M were lent to Canada from Germany and deployed to Afghanistan in August 2007. The Barracuda Technologies Mobile Camouflage System (MCS) was added in March/April 2008. The tank is painted in a standard three-colour NATO camouflage under the MCS, while the slat armour is in CARC Tan.

LEOPARD 2A6

PANZERBATAILLON 104, 10. PANZERDIVISION, BUNDESWEHR, GERMANY 2012.

1/35 SCALE
BORDER MODELS
DAVID GRUMMITT

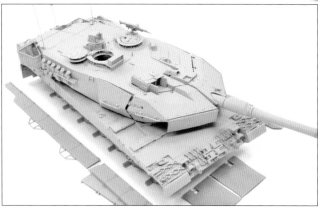

(left) The Border Model kit is crisply moulded and very accurate. The instructions, however, could be clearer, so take care! The kit can be assembled as a Leopard 2A5, Leopard 2A6 early or Leopard 2A6 late. I chose the latter option.

(below left) Bundeswehr Leopard 2s have a sprayed standard NATO camouflage scheme with a fine-edged demarcations of colour. I drew the pattern first with an AK Interactive water-soluble pencil.

(below) Over the base colour of NATO Green I masked around the areas that would be sprayed NATO Black using Silly Putty. The Silly Putty gives a very good result avoiding the completely hard-edged pattern that would result in using masking tape. The same was then done for the NATO Brown and any errors were corrected using the airbrush freehand.

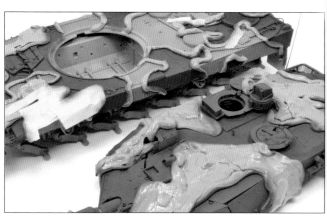

(above) The sprayed pattern: I then applied an Olive Green filter just to tie the three colours together and form the base for the subsequent weathering.

(above right) The camouflage netting came from Tetra Model Works. It needs soaking in white glue before attaching to the model. The pine boughs from Mantis Miniatures provide the final touch.

A heavily camouflaged Leopard 2A6 of Panzerbataillon 104 crosses the Grafenwoehr Training Area during Exercise Iron Panzer in December 2011. (US Army photo by Gertrud Zach)

(above) Italeri 243

(above)Revell 03060

MODELLING PRODUCTS

Since the mid 1980s the Leopard 2 has been a hugely popular subject among modellers and kit manufacturers alike, with a range of models covering almost all the major variants in a variety of scales. The aim of this section is to survey the available kits and accessories and provide some helpful advice to modellers who wish to tackle their own Leopard 2 project from my own experience and by synthesising the comments and experience of others.

1/35-SCALE KITS

The Leopard 2 was first kitted in 1/35 scale by Italeri back in 1985 (ref. 243). This was quite a good kit for its day, but it is certainly now showing its age. It represents a Leopard 2A2 or A3 and contains markings for two Bundeswehr and one Dutch vehicle. The Italeri kit was the basis for related releases by Esci (ref. 5022, 5023 and 5030, which also contains fourteen soft-plastic 'NATO soldiers'), Heller (ref. 81139), Testors (ref. 820), Matchbox (ref. 3502) and Revell (03053). All these kits differ in small details and provide different marking options but they are, essentially, the 1985 Italeri kit reboxed.

Italeri's kit also provided the basis for the first Leopard 2A5 kits, released in the early 1990s. Italeri's Leopard II Improved/KWS Version (ref. 280) represents one of the two prototype KWS Leopard 2s. This was re-released in 1998 (ref. 365) as a production Leopard 2A5 and also subsequently reboxed by Academy (ref. 13282). In 2006 Revell supplemented their Leopard 2A5 with a 2A6 (ref. 03060). In 2000 Tamiya released their version of the Leopard 2A5 (ref. 35242). This was developed in association with Krauss-Maffei and was, and still is,

a superb kit. Three years later Tamiya followed this up with a Leopard 2A6 (ref. 35271).Tamiya's kits are basically accurate and very easy to build and can form the basis of a range of Leopard 2 variants.

In 2012 Revell released a newly tooled Leopard 2A6/A6M (ref. 03097). This is an excellent kit that includes the extra belly armour and new 6/2 smoke discharger array. It led to a range of new Revell Leopard 2 kits: a Leopard 2A4/2NL (ref. 03193), a Leopard 2A5/2A5NL (ref. 03243), a Leopard 2A6/A6NL (ref. 03281) and Leopard 2A7 (ref. 03273). These Revell kits are, on the whole, very good. They are straightforward to build and have a good variety of markings and optional parts, but are not without issues (the non-skid texture is not wholly accurate, for instance, on the newly tooled Leopard 2A4/2NL).

In 2006 modellers of the Leopard 2 were greeted with a range of new kits from Chinese-manufacturer Hobbyboss. These included a Leopard 2A4 (ref. 82401), a Leopard 2A5/A6 (ref. 82402), Leopard 2A6EX (ref. 82403), Strv. 122 (ref. 82404) and Leopard 2A5DK (ref. 82405), followed two years later by a Leopard 2A5/A6NL (ref. 82423), in 2009 by a Leopard 2E (ref. 82432) and in 2010, by a Leopard 2A6M CAN (ref. 82458). These kits are, to the say the least, something of a mixed bag. The first two to be released, the Leopard 2A5DK and Strv. 122, were pretty poor, suffering from inaccurate

(above) Tamiya 35271
(right) Revell 03281

(above) Hobbyboss 82404

(above) Hobbyboss 83867

details, poorly rendered weld seams, and overdone anti-skid surfaces. They appeared to be rather poor copies of the HKCW resin conversions designed for the Tamiya kit. The thick anti-skid panels also marred the Leopard 2A5NL/A6NL release, while the Leopard 2E and 2A6EX are best ignored as they bear little resemblance to the real vehicles, but other kits in this range by Hobbyboss are better. The Leopard 2A4 has the thickness of the anti-skid surfaces reduced, for instance, but its details are still a little soft compared to the new Revell tooling or the latest Meng Model kit. The Leopard 2A6M CAN includes the slat armour fitted to these vehicles, allowing you to represent a tank prior to the fitting of the Barracuda MCS in 2008. Hobbyboss somewhat redeemed their reputation among Leopard 2 modellers in 2015 when they released a newly tooled Leopard 2A4M CAN (ref. 83867). This is an excellent kit that gives a range of options. Interestingly, although it comes with a very good set of slat amour, no mention is made that this slat armour is not usually fitted to the tanks (indeed, it was only fitted during their very limited service in Afghanistan). One startling, but very welcome, feature of the kit is the inclusion of no fewer than 506 tiny decals to represent the velcro strips used to fit the MCS. The most obvious error, something carried over from their older Leopard 2 kits, is that that the rear engine grillee has twelve slats instead of the eleven on the real thing. Despite that Hobbyboss's Leopard 2A4M CAN is a very good kit comparable to Tamiya's Leopard 2s, only

surpassed by the latest releases from Meng Model and Border Models.

In 2015 Meng Model released a Leopard 2A4 (ref. TS-016) which set a new standard for Leopard 2 kits in 1/35 scale. This really is a superb kit. Built out of the box it will best represent a fifth-series Bundeswehr vehicle, but there are a number of options, not all identified in the instructions, possible. The kit includes both the early and late-style heavy side skirts, but it is possible to depict either the early pattern (batches 1-5), the front three sections replaced with the heavy pattern skirts (batches 6-7) and the late-pattern skirts identical to those developed for the Leopard 2A5/A6 (batch 8). The turret loading hatch is welded shut, but the weld seam can easily be sanded off for the final production batches. One of the best features of this kit are the individual track links. A jig is provided to assemble these and no glue is required meaning the tracks are fully workable. One thing to note is Meng's workable torsion bar suspension. These are prone to sag with the weight of the model - see my own build of the kit in the gallery – and should be fixed ideally to allow the model to sit at the right height. Another thing to watch are the three reinforcing strips at the bottom of the rear hull; these were not fitted to Bundeswehr Leopard 2A4s. Meng followed this release with a Leopard 2A7 (ref. TS-027). Again, this is a superb kit and, although it shares some sprues (such as the suspension and tracks) in common with the Leopard 2A4, it is largely newly tooled plastic. The upper hull is completely new and includes the specific APU of the Leopard 2A7, while the additional armour for the lower hull is faithfully reproduced. There are some great details in this kit, such as the touch-screen monitor for the Rocky RK9 component of the IFIS (see the image on p. 13). The third Meng Model Leopard 2 kit is the Leopard 2A7+ (ref. TS-042). This is the demonstrator vehicle developed by KMW to demonstrate the urban

(above, right) Meng Model TS-027. The individual-link tracks, included in all three of Meng Model's Leopard 2 kits, are superb and easy to assemble with the help of the kit-supplied jig.

The details of Border Model's Leopard 2A5/A6 (BT-002) are evident from this in-progress image from the author's build of this kit

operations potential of the Leopard 2. This kit contains the new armour packages and the RWS and, needless to say, is superb all round.

A similarly themed release to this latter Meng kit is Tiger Models' Leopard 2 Revolution. This was a technology demonstrator developed by Rheinmetall and comes in two versions the Revolution 1 (ref. 4629) and Revolution 2 (ref. 4628). The real tank includes a heavily modified armour package for the export market, which is faithfully replicated in the kit. This means that it can only be built in the Revolution configuration, so while this is an excellent kit it has little relevance for modellers of the Leopard 2 in service with NATO countries and elsewhere.

The latest manufacturer to enter the market with a Leopard 2 kit in 1/35 scale is Border Model. This Leopard 2A5/A6 (ref. BT-002) is the second kit released by this manufacturer (the first being a Panzer IV) and they have made quite an entry with what is almost certainly the best Leopard 2 kit on the market. The basic accuracy and 'buildability' of this kit is second to none and it provides a good range of options to build the Leopard 2A5/A6 as seen in Bundeswehr and Polish service. Different smoke discharger and side skirt configurations are included, as are photoetched parts and individual track links. The weakest part of the kit is probably the marking options:

(below) Tiger Model 4628

the Bundeswehr markings are incomplete, while the Polish Leopard 2A6 is, of course, entirely fictional. Modellers of the Leopard 2 are exceptionally well served in 1/35 scale, with the latest generation of kits by Meng and Border being among the most accurate and most buildable injection-moulded kits on the market. All we need now is a latest-generation plastic kit of the Leopard 2HEL!

1/16 AND 1/48-SCALE KITS

In 2004 Tamiya released a 'full option' 1/16-scale kit of the Leopard 2A6 (ref. 56020). The model is a radio-controlled tank, primarily designed for the R/C enthusiasts, but, as it is based on Tamiya's 1/35-scale kit, it's a pretty good replica of the Leopard 2A6. The tracks are perfect replicas of the real thing, with individual rubber track pads, while the mesh of the rear turret stowage baskets and the cooling fan grillees on the engine deck can be replaced with photoetched parts. The price, however, will probably deter most military modellers as the kit is only available in the full R/C option.

The Leopard 2 has been largely ignored by Quarterscale modellers and manufacturers and only Academy have kitted the tank in plastic. Sadly, Academy's radio-controlled kits (refs. 13310, 13008 and 1304) are very toy-like and do stand up to scrutiny by serious military modellers. French-firm Gaso.Line have a complete kit of the Leopard 2A5/A6 (ref. GAS50258) in resin, with vinyl tracks and some photoetched details. The dimensions are basically accurate and it has a nicely reproduced anti-slip texture, but some of the details are a little soft. Nevertheless with some work this will build into a fine replica.

(above and right) Hasegawa's 31134: note the awful single-piece tracks and suspension!

1/72-SCALE KITS

The range of kits and accessories available to modellers wanting to start a Small-Scale Leopard 2 project is not as wide as that in the larger scale of 1/35 but it is still extensive. The first serious Small-Scale Leopard 2 was released by Hasegawa back in 1986 (ref. MA2) and re-released, as Leopard 2A4, in 1995 (ref. 31134). While dimensionally reasonably accurate, this kit is not really up to today's standards. Although some of the detail (such as the engine deck and anti-slip surfaces) are quite sharp, it has moulded on turret handholds and the tracks and wheels are, quite inexplicably, moulded as a single piece. The kit represents a very early Leopard 2 with the turret crosswind sensor and, interestingly, it also includes the snorkel equipment for the commander's cupola fitted during early deep-wading exercises. In 1994 Matchbox released a 1/72-scale Leopard 2A4 (ref. 40182), which was subsequently reboxed by Revell (ref. 03103 and, as a Leopard 2A5, ref. 03105) and Monogram (ref. 2322). This is quite a nice kit, although some of the detail is a little heavy and its overall dimensions come up a little on the small side. It has the advantage over the Hasegawa kit of link-and-length tracks. It's fair to say

though that the level of detail is not up to the standard modellers would expect from contemporary kits. Note too that Revell didn't modify the hull to represent the new-style driver's hatch in their 2A5 version of this kit.

In 2006 Dragon Model Limited released a Leopard 2A6 (ref. 7232) in their 1/72 scale Armor Pro series. At the time of its release this was the best Small-Scale Leopard 2 available and is still a very good kit. The kit provides both the L/44 and L/55 main guns and a choice of side skirts, enabling the modeller to build either the Leopard 2A5 or 2A6 out of the box. The KWS II turret armour is very well done as separate panels, while the anti-skid surfaces are nicely represented. The suspension is very good, but the one-piece vinyl tracks are less convincing than the link-and-length alternatives offered in some other kits. The pioneer tools are moulded on, but all the hatches are supplied as separate pieces. The following year Dragon released a Leopard 2A4 (ref. 7249) based on the same moulds. Again, this is a lovely kit, with a redesigned upper hull with the correct, older-style driver's hatch for the Leopard 2A4. A range of markings options are given for German, Dutch, Polish, Finnish and Swiss tanks, but unfortunately none of the country-specific modifications (such as the smoke dischargers or turret stowage boxes) are included and the kit can only properly be built as a Bundeswehr vehicle.

Probably the best injection-moulded Leopard 2 available now is the newly tooled kit by Revell kit, first released in 2011. To date there are three versions available: the Leopard 2A6/A6M (ref. 03180), the Leopard 2A5/A5NL (ref. 03187) and the Strv. 122A/122B (ref. 03199). All these kits are distinguished by an overall accuracy, crisp moulding and a nice attention to detail. The suspension is busy, but the tracks are moulded as two single runs of plastic which need to be softened in hot water and bent

(left) Matchbox 40182

(bottom left) Dragon 7232

(below) Dragon 7249

(top left) Revell 03180
(left and above) Revell 03199

round the roadwheels, idler and drive sprocket. This is easier than it sounds and the end result is very good. The belly armour for the Leopard 2A6M is included, but a few of the details for this newer variant (such as the tow cable clips on the rear hull) are missing. The Dutch version includes the correct smoke dischargers and the loader's FN machine gun, as well as the additional turret roof stowage box frequently seen on Dutch tanks. Similarly, the Strv. 122 contains the additional hull frontal armour the distinctive turret stowage boxes of the Swedish Leopard 2.

In 2019 Chinese-firm Modelcollect announced they were releasing a 1/72-scale kit of the Leopard 2A6 (ref. 72120). Modelcollect has a strong reputation for Small-Scale armour kits, especially modern Soviet and Russian subject, so their Leopard 2 should be a good kit. There seems to have been a delay in the release of this kit, which was announced in 2019, and sadly it now seems to have disappeared from their catalogue. There are a few full resin kits of the Leopard 2 available, such as the Leopard 2A5NL (ref. MT72105) by Modell Trans Modellbau, but these have been superseded by the kits now available in plastic or are now out of production.

REPLACEMENT TRACKS

The tracks on early Leopard 2 kits in both 1/35 and Small-Scale were pretty poor. The Esci and Italeri kits, as well as the newer Tamiya, 1/35-scale kits came with single-piece vinyl efforts and the early Small-Scale efforts are best forgotten. There are a range of replacement tracks available, however, in both scales. The first workable plastic track links in 1/35 scale were released in 2000 by H.K. Creation Workshop (ref. TL 3502) and these are basically the same as the Trumpeter Type 570P 'Diehl' Tracks (ref. 02039), as are those released by AFV Club (ref. AS35S09). These are excellent and a great improvement over the vinyl Italeri or Tamiya kits, but perhaps not quite up to the standard of the individual links included in Meng Model's Leopard 2 kits. In 2010 Bronco Models released a set of Leopard 2 MBT Workable Track Links (ref. AB3528). Unfortunately these are slightly out of scale and require you to adjust the sprocket teeth of the Tamiya and other kits for a perfect fit. For those modellers who prefer the weight of metal tracks links, these are available from Easy Metal Links (ref. EML35-004), Friul Model (ref. ATL-159), and R Model (ref. 35182R). In resin, Leopard Workshop also

have a set of Diehl 570PO tracks and sprockets (ref. LW031) as latterly fitted to the Leopard 2A5DK. In Small-Scale there is an excellent set of replacement resin tracks and sprockets available from OKB Grigorov, as well as a 3-D printed set by J-Shape Works (ref. JS72T001).

CONVERSION AND DETAIL SETS: LEOPARD WORKSHOP

As we have seen the range of Leopard 2 variants and production changes introduced during their long service history has spawned an array of conversion and detailing sets available for 1/35-scale plastic kits. Two companies in particular – Leopard Workshop and Perfect Scale Modellbau – produce a range of resin, metal and photoetched sets that provide a wealth of options to modellers of the Leopard 2 (and the Leopard 1).

Leopard Workshop break down their kits into a number of helpful categories on their website which makes finding the correct detailing set or accessory easy. First, they offer major conversions to existing plastic kits. Their Leopard 2A6M+ conversion (ref. LW037) offers the mine belly armour plate and Ultra-Cap behind the commander's cupola to update the Tamiya or any of the existing Leopard 2A6 kits. There are also a set of 'Velcro' Patches for the Leopard 2A4M CAN (ref. LW035) which are three-dimensional and an improvement over the decals supplied in the Hobby Boss kit. There is also an extensive resin and photoetched conversion kit for Tamiya's Leopard 2A6 to the 2017 version of the Leopard 2A6M CAN (ref. LW040). Another additional accessory is a resin FN MAG/C6 machine gun (ref. LW047), as used on Dutch Leopard 2s, which is a great improvement over the plastic version available in the Revell kits.

Leopard Workshop also offer a range of replacement multi-part resin barrels for 1/35-scale kits. These are an improvement over the kit parts, not only because they are the correct length but they also offer alternative fume extractors, including the rough cast fibreglass variety which are absent from the plastic kits. These are Leopard 2A4 L/44 barrels for the Revell (ref. LW017R), Meng (ref. LW017M), Hobby Boss (ref. LW17HB) and Tiger Model (ref. LW017REV) kits, as well as Leopard 2A5/A6 barrels for Revell (ref. LW018R), and Tamiya and Hobby Boss (ref. LW018T). There is also a replacement barrel, with the three alternative fume extractors, for the Meng Leopard 2A7 kit (ref. LW018M). One of the weakest points of the existing plastic Leopard 2 kits are the smoke discharger arrays and, again, Leopard Workshop have come to the rescue with a selection of correct aligned and proportioned smoke dischargers, complete with photoetched retaining chains. These include both the 4+4 (ref. LW027A) and 6+2 (ref. LW027B) arrangements, as well as the dischargers manufactured by KMW specifically for production batch 8 of the Leopard 2A4 (ref. LW027C). There are also available a range of other details, including Rear Mud Flaps (ref. LW030), Mantlet Plugs (ref. LW004), photoetched turret basket mesh for the Tamiya kit (ref. LW043), and a set of replacement roadwheels with correct detailing on the inner face (ref. LW013).

One of the most useful ranges offered by Leopard Workshop are their replacement radio aerials. These cover all the major systems employed on the Leopard 2 by both Germany and other NATO countries. They include: Canadian Aerials for Leopard 2A4M and 2A6M CAN (ref. LW015B), US-Style AS-1729 aerials (ref. LW012B), SEM80/90 aerials (ref. LW024) and Comrod aerials (ref. LW034B). They include photoetch, turned metal bases, flexible springs and turned metal antenna and are a massive improvement over what is consistently

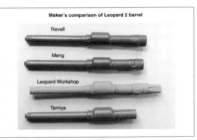

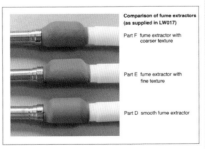

(above) LW018T 2A5/2A6 Gun Barrel for Tamiya/Hobby Boss

(below) LW024 SEM80/90 aerials

(above left) LW037 Leopard 2A6M+ conversion

(above) information sheet from LW017 and LW018 barrel and fume extractor sets

(left) LW027C smoke launchers

one of the weaker aspects of any plastic kit.

CONVERSION AND DETAIL SETS: PERFECT SCALE MODELLBAU

The other company offering an extensive range of resin accessories, conversions and detail sets for the Leopard 2 are the German firm Perfect Scale Modellbau. In terms of major conversions, these include a number of sets for Canadian Leopard 2s: a Leopard 2A4M CAN (ref. 35082) and Leopard 2A6M CAN (ref. 35071) both with Barracuda MCS. Both include replacement upper hulls and turrets with the MCS in place. There is also a separate resin and photoetched set to improve Hobby Boss's Leopard 2A6M CAN (ref. 35068). There are also two extensive resin sets to convert the Revell or Meng Leopard 2A4 to the Stridsvagn 121A (ref. 35152) or Stridsvagn 121B (ref. 35156). As far as Bundeswehr Leopard 2s are concerned, we have a set for enhancing the detail on Meng's already excellent Leopard 2A7 (ref. 35169) and for converting the Tamiya kit to the Leopard 2A6MA2 (or 2A6M+) (ref. 35179) or 2A6M (ref. 35014).

Perfect Scale Modellbau also have an extensive range of resin accessories to upgrade or replace inaccurate or poorly detailed parts from the plastic kits. These include 6+2 (ref. 35013) and 4+4 smoke dischargers (ref. 35044), an early version L/44 gun (ref. 35041), Leopard 2A0 – 2A4 side skirts (ref. 35043), the rubber matting designed to hang from the turret and hull to disguise the tank's thermal signature (ref. 35060), 'new style' side skirts for the Leopard 2A5/A6 (ref. 35061), a new engine grille to replace the inaccurate one included in Hobby Boss' Leopard 2A4M CAN (ref. 35159), worn roadwheels (ref. 35167), T-shape towing hooks (ref. 35166), the 'Darkas' mount used on the Leopard 2A5 to 2A7 (ref. 35172), protection bars for the front hull indicator lights

(ref. 35177), and a generic set of photoetched parts (ref PE004).

Also in the Perfect Scale Modellbau catalogue is a complete Leopard 2 powerpack and engine compartment This is a complex resin kit designed to fit into any of the Tamiya or Hobby Boss kits. They are available separately as Leopard 2 Power Pack (ref. 35005) and Engine Compartment (ref. 35006), and as a combination (ref. 35001). The engine compartment is designed for the Tamiya or Hobby Boss kit and some surgery and extra work will be required to make it fit the latest Meng kits but the engine itself is a wonderful replica and, although one for the modeller experienced working with resin, will certainly result in an eye-catching model.

Perfect Scale Modellbau also have an extensive range of resin accessories to upgrade or replace inaccurate or poorly detailed parts from the plastic kits. These include 6+2 (ref. 35013) and 4+4 smoke dischargers (ref. 35044), an early version L/44 gun (ref. 35041), Leopard 2A0 – 2A4 side skirts (ref. 35043), the rubber matting designed to hang from the turret and hull to disguise the tank's thermal signature (ref. 35060), 'new style' side skirts for the Leopard 2A5/A6 (ref. 35061), a new engine grille to replace the inaccurate one included in Hobby Boss' Leopard 2A4M CAN (ref. 35159), worn roadwheels (ref. 35167), T-shape towing hooks (ref. 35166), the 'Darkas' mount used on the Leopard 2A5 to 2A7 (ref. 35172), protection bars for the front hull indicator lights (ref. 35177), and a generic set of photoetched parts (ref. PE004). Their latest release is a SPECTUS for the Leopard 2A7 (ref. 35200). This new system from Airbus replaces the driver's night sight and includes five nicely cast resin pieces that simply fit in place on the Meng Model kit.

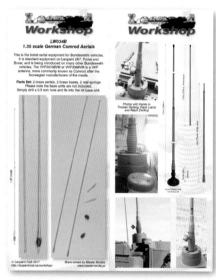

(above) Leopard Workshop
LW034B Comrod aerials

Perfect Scale Modellbau
(top) 35169
(above) 35006
(left) 35179
(top right) 35013
(right) 35001

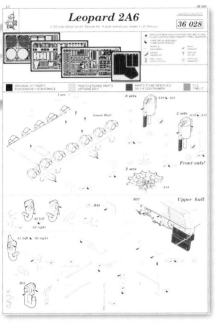

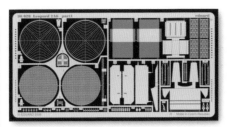

(left and above) 36028 - Eduard's photoetch is relatively simple and a great introduction if you are new to modelling in this medium.

(above) E.T Model EA35-115
(left and below) E.T Model EA35-254

Voyager's sets are on a completely different level, requiring great skill and patience to replace much of the plastic kit with photoetch, resin and brass.

(below) Voyager Model PE35776   *(below) Voyager Model PE35774*

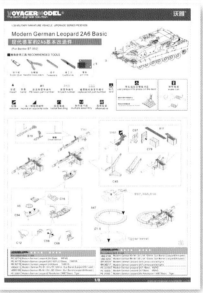

(right) Voyager Model PE351026

ACCESSORIES: PHOTOETCHED DETAIL PARTS

Unsurprisingly, there is a plethora of different photoetched detail sets available for the Leopard 2 in 1/35 scale. Czech-firm Eduard were one of the pioneers of using photoetched brass to enhance plastic kits. Their sets are designed principally for the older plastic kits as more recently the company's efforts have been directed towards their own range of aircraft kits and detail sets. Eduard's photoetch sets tend to be relatively simple compared to some of the newer names on the market and suffer from the two-dimensional appearance that is inevitable in photoetched details sets. Nevertheless, their sets are well worth looking at, especially if you are simply looking for turret basket mesh, engine deck grillees and the like to update the otherwise excellent Tamiya kits. They produce simple update sets containing these grillees for the Tamiya Leopard 2A5 (ref. TP008) and Leopard 2A6 (refs. TP080, 36028), as well as more complete sets for the various Italeri kits (refs. 35302, 35340, 35974). They also produce a series of sets designed for the Hobby Boss Leopard 2A6M CAN (refs. 36182, 36183, 36184). The slat armour is also available adapted for use on the Tamiya Leopard 2A6 (ref. 36019). Now discontinued, Eduard did produce a 'Big Ed' set for the Tamiya Leopard 2A6 kit, including a detail set, the slat armour and a set of wheel and periscope vinyl masks (ref. BIG3561). These masks, which are a handy solution to one of the most time-consuming aspects of any modern armour build are also available separately (refs. XT036, XT079).

Typical of the 'new generation' photoetched detail sets are those produced by the Chinese-manufacturer E.T.

Model. They produce a range of sets designed for Tamiya, but also for the newer Meng and Tiger Model kits. German Leopard 2A5/A6 MBT Engine & Turret Rack Grillees (ref. EA35-115) are a neat little set that will immediately enhance the appearance of the Tamiya's Leopard 2, while they also offer a more comprehensive set for the Tamiya kits (ref. EA35-239). They also produce sets for the Meng Leopard 2A4 (ref. EA35-240), Leopard 2A7 (ref. EA35-254) and the Tiger Model's Leopard 2 Revolution (ref. EA35-261).

The other big name in detail sets is, of course, Voyager Model. Voyager's detail sets tend to also include resin and other 3D parts and tend to be more comprehensive, and correspondingly more demanding, than those of other manufacturers. They produce a range of sets, from the very simple (grillees for the Tamiya kit, refs. AP006, AP007, FE35008) to the very complex. These include sets for the major kits from Border, Meng Tamiya and Tiger Model. These are available both as a 'basic' photoetched detail set and as a set with a resin and turned metal gun barrel included (Meng Leopard 2A7, refs. PE351007, PE35859; Border Model, refs. PE351025 for Leopard 2A5, PE351026 for Leopard 2A6; Tamiya Leopard 2A5, refs. PE35775A, PE35775B; Tamiya Leopard 2A6, refs. PE35776A, PE35776B; Meng Leopard 2A4, ref. PE35774; Tiger Model Leopard 2 Revolution, refs.

PE35890, PE35891). As well as these sets, Voyager offer their barrels separately, and also a very useful set of coloured headlight and tail lights for the Meng Model kits (Leopard 2A4, ref. BR35024 and Leopard 2A7, ref. BR35217, newly tooled as BR35227). Finally, there are separately available side skirts for the Meng Leopard 2A4 (ref. PEA363), and for the Leopard 2A5/A6 (ref. PEA442), as well as the DARKAS training simulator for both the Leopard 2A5/A6/A7 and Leopard 2A4 (ref. PEA443). One another manufacturer worth noting is Korean-firm Tetra Model Works who produce a comprehensive set to enhance the Tamiya kit (ref. ME-35018).

SMALL-SCALE PHOTOETCH

E.T. Model produce a couple of good photoetch detail sets for the Revell and Dragon Small-Scale Leopard 2A5/A6. These are notable as they include replacement additional frontal turret armour (Revell ref. E72-002, Dragon E72-027). Eduard produced a set to detail the older Small-Scale Revell Leopard 2A4 (ref. 22016), while Extratech made generic sets containing grillees and other details (Leopard 2A4, ref. EXV 72021, Leopard 2A5, ref. EXV 72017, and Leopard 2A6, ref.EXV 72098). Probably the best value 1/72-scale photoetched detail sets are the two made by Hauler, one for Dragon's Leopard 2A6 (ref. HLH72080) and Leopard 2A4 (ref. HLH72082).

OTHER ACCESSORIES AND CONVERSIONS

There are a range of other manufacturers in 1/35 scale who offer resin and photoetched accessories and conversions for the Leopard 2 modeller. Most of these are designed to replace or improve inaccurate or poorly detailed plastic kit parts, but some offer versions of the Leopard 2 not available in plastic. Czech-firm Real Model offer a range of accessories and details set, specifically for

the Leopard 2A6M CAN. These are designed to convert the Tamiya kit and include both types of slat armour (refs. RM35149 and RM35150) and conversion sets that reflect the different upgrades and configurations the Leopard 2A6M CAN has seen during its service (refs. RM35158, RM35159). There are also sets designed to correct the Hobby Boss kit (refs. RM35159 and RM35219), as well as a detail set for the Leopard 2A4M CAN (ref. RM35277). Real Model also produce engine sets designed for the Italeri (ref. RMA35107) and Tamiya kits (ref. RMA35037). In a similar vein, Black Dog also produce a complete replacement resin turret and hull with Barracuda MCS for the Hobby Boss Leopard 2A6M CAN (ref. T35039). Another notable resin conversion is Accurate Armour's for the Leopard 2A5DK. They offer two comprehensive resin and photoetched detail sets, one for the Tamiya kit (ref. C101) and one to update the Hobby Boss kit (ref. C102). These have been produced in cooperation with Thomas Antonsen and are both accurate and produced to a very high standard. Legend Productions also produce two useful detailing sets: the first, for the Leopard 2A5/A6NL contains smoke dischargers, FN MAG, storage boxes and other details that are a big improvement over the plastic parts in the various Revell kits (ref. LF1121) and, second, a detailing set for the Leopard 2A4M CAN (ref. LF1342).

The final resin manufacturer worth mentioning is the German-firm Y-Modelle. To some extent these conversions, largely based on the Hobby Boss with all their attendant issues, have been superseded by the latest generation of Meng Model's kits, but they are worth having a look at it you have the opportunity. They include a Leopard 2A7+ conversion for Hobby Boss's Leopard 2A6EX (ref. Y35-148), Leopard 2A7 for Hobby Boss's Leopard 2A5/A6 (ref. Y35-138), a Leopard 2A7+

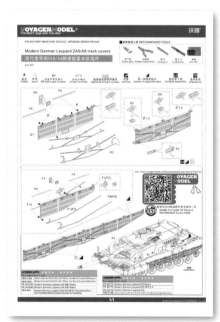

(above) Voyager Model BR35217

(above) E.T Model E72-002

(below) RM35149. Real Model's sets for the Leopard 2A6M CAN
are a comprehensive mixture of resin and photoetched parts.

(above) Voyager Model PEA442
(below) Hauler HLH72081

conversion for Hobby Boss's Leopard 2A5DK (ref. Y35-115), and an update for the Leopard 2A4M CAN (ref. Y35-119). They also do a range of conversions for the Wisent II armoured recovery/armoured engineer vehicle and Leguan bridgelayer.

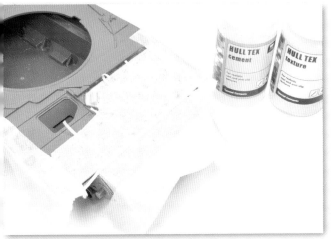

(left) C101. The Accurate Armour Leopard 2A5DK conversion for the Tamiya kit contains the add-on frontal armour. Here I am in the process of adding the non-slip texture using the excellent products from VMS.

(below) Black Dog T35039

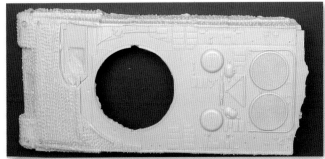

DECALS

As is clear from the colour profiles and photographs in this volume, the Leopard 2 is a colourful beast with a variety of different camouflage finishes, tactical and national markings. A number of aftermarket producers have released 1/35-scale decals for the Leopard 2. Premier among them is probably Singapore-based company Echelon Fine Details. There decal sets are well-researched with clear instructions on placement and the decals themselves beautifully produced with little carrier film and the colours in perfect register. Two sets cover the Swedish Strv. 122 (refs. T35003, T35007, the latter covering the named tanks of the Norbotten Regiment); there is also a set for the Spanish Leopard 2A4 (ref. T35001); and 'Fearsome Cats of the European Nations' (ref. T35008), which covers Greek, Polish, Finnish, Norwegian, Swedish and Danish tanks. Two sets cover Canadian Leopard 2s: Canadian Leopard 2A6M (ref. D356044) and RCAC & RCD Gagetown Leopard Tanks (ref. D356221). As well as these markings sets, Echelon also produce silver, orange and red reflectors for use on Swedish tanks (ref. D356035, D356083, D356084).

Spanish-firm FC Modeltips have an extensive sheet covering both the Leopard 2A4 and Leopard 2E (ref. FCM35027), while LM Decals have two sheets for the Greek Leopard 2, including one the attractive tenth-anniversary livery applied to the Leopard 2HEL (refs. LMX 008, LM 35015). The anniversary livery is printed to order and can be reproduced in any scale, and should be combined with LM 35015. TL-Decals produce sets for the Norwegian (ref. 2586) and Austrian (ref. 2588) Leopard 2, while ToRo Model produce a range of decals covering various Leopard 2A4 and 2A5 in Polish service (refs. 35D01, 35D21, 35D24, 35D55, 35D64). Finally, Black Lion Decals produce a set with the logo 'Trots op onze jongens' (Proud of our Boys') which was applied to two Leopard 2A6NL of 42 Tankbataljon in 2008 to mark the Euro 2008 football championship and the Dutch contribution to ISAF (ref. BLD05-2010).

In 1/72 scale Black Lion Decals produce two sets for the Leopard 2: one for export users, including markings for Chilean, Greek, Norwegian, Austrian, Spanish, Danish, Swedish and Swiss tanks (ref. 72043) and another for Dutch Leopard 2s (ref. 72035). LM Decals have a set for Greek Leopards (ref. 72010), while ToRo Model have a range of three sets (refs. 72D01, 72D22, 72D47) covering Polish tanks.

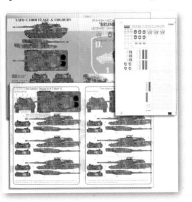

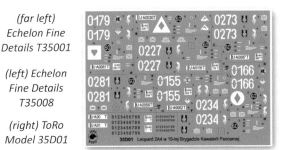

(far left) Echelon Fine Details T35001

(left) Echelon Fine Details T35008

(right) ToRo Model 35D01

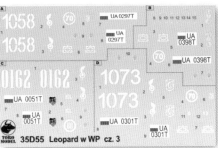

(left) ToRo Model 35D55

(right Black Lion Decals 72043

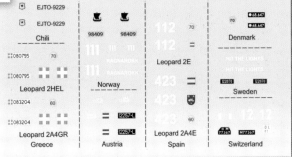

.text continued from page 15...

Recovery Vehicles (ARVs) to Canada. A series of modifications, principally the addition of slat armour to defeat Rocket-Propelled Grenades (RPGs), were applied at KMW in the summer of 2007 before the tanks arrived in theatre between July and September that year. In the meantime the Canadians had negotiated the purchase of a eighty surplus Leopard 2A4s and twenty Leopard 2A6NL from the Netherlands. Forty of the Leopard 2A4 arrived in Montreal in November 2008, while the remainder were delivered to KMW for modification to Leopard 2A4M CAN standard. These were delivered to the Canadian army in October 2010 and five tanks so configured were deployed to Kandahar Province that December. As we will see, the Leopard 2A4M CAN and Leopard 2A6M CAN played an important role in ISAF's operations before the cessation of combat operations in July 2011. Some of the Leopard 2s deployed to Afghanistan underwent a major repair and rebuild at KMW, but forty Leopard 2A4s which had arrived in Canada were brought up to Canadian specifications at Rheinmetall's facility in Saint-Jean-sur-Richelieu, Québec. In the spring of 2012 the Leopard 2A4M CAN entered service with units stationed in Canada. In October the following year, the twenty rebuilt Leopard 2A6M, splendid in their new CARC Green paint were delivered to the Royal Canadian Armored School in Oromocto, New Brunswick. In repayment of these vehicles, the Canadian government had the twenty Leopard 2A6NL purchased in 2008 sent to KMW for upgrade to Leopard 2A6M standard before being delivered to the Bundeswehr. Canada's fleet of Leopard 2s are currently in service with three armoured regiments, comprising a squadron in the Royal Canadian Dragoons (shared with 12e Régiment blindé du Canada) and two squadrons of Lord Strathcona's Horse (Royal Canadians).

The Leopard 2A4M CAN and 2A6M CAN have a number of unique modifications. Initially, the Leopard 2A6M CAN deployed to Afghanistan had full slat armour, additional glacis plate protection, cooling vests for the crew instead of an air-conditioning unit, Canadian radios and T-shaped antenna, a turret roof-mounted C8 Carbine box for the crew's small arms, and an additional stowage box behind the commander's cupola. While in Afghanistan other modifications were added, including removing the bottom three or four rails of the slat armour as they were frequently damaged and introducing an camouflage netting 'umbrella' that protected the commander from the heat of the Afghan sun. On their refurbishment following the end of their tour in Afghanistan, the Leopard 2A6M CAN was also fitted with the driver's rear-view camera. The Leopard 2A4M CAN was similarly equipped but with a shorter version of the slat armour and additional turret armour similar to that found on the Leopard 2A7+. Both were equipped for the Barracuda MCS. Not all Leopard 2A4s have been upgraded to 2A4M standard and these tanks lack the additional turret armour but have other Canadian modifications, including replacing the Dutch-style smoke dischargers with standard German 6+2 configuration. The Leopard 2A4 CAN and 2A4M CAN are also fitted with two FN C6 7.62mm machine guns. In their current configuration with units in Canada both the Leopard 2A4M CAN and 2A6M CAN have had the slat armour removed (although the former retains the velcro attachment points for the Barracuda MCS). The Leopard 2A4M CAN and Leopard 2A6M CAN also have fittings for a variety of mine plough/roller and dozer blade attachments.

A Leopard 2A4 of 12e Régiment blindé du Canada/Royal Canadian Dragoons during Exercise Common Ground at the 5th Canadian Division Support Base Gagetown, New Brunswick, in November 2019. (Cpl. Cayer, 2e Bataillon Royal 22e Régiment)

DENMARK

In the early 1990s Denmark decided to replace its Leopard 1 and Centurion fleet with a third-generation MBT, like the Leopard 2. Denmark had recent experience of fielding MBTs and Leopard 1A5DKs been deployed to Bosnia as part of the NATO mission there, where they had gained valuable combat experience. In December 1997 the Danes procured 51 Leopard 2A4 from Bundeswehr stocks at a cost of some 100 million Euros. In 2004 a further six Leopard 2A4s were bought, followed by eighteen to be used as spares the following year. The Leopard 2A4 had a short service life with the Danish Army, serving in an unmodified specification, as preparation for the future developments of the Danish armoured force.

From the beginning the Danes, building upon the combat experience they had gained in Bosnia, wished to upgrade the Leopard 2A4. In 2000 the Danes received a single standard Leopard 2A5 to begin familiarisation with the latest variant of the tank. The Danes opted to upgrade their Leopard 2A4 to the KWS II standard and retain compatibility with the Leopard 2s of the LEOBEN association nations (Leopard Benützer Nationen). In June 2000 a contract was signed to upgrade the 51 Leopard 2A4 to A5 standard. Two important changes were introduced on top of the KWS II specifications: first, additional frontal armour, similar to that fitted to the Swedish Stridsvagn 122 was fitted and, second, an Auxiliary Power Unit, based on Danish experiences in Bosnia, was installed. A number of other external changes were introduced including new rear turret stowage bins, 'six plus two' smoke dischargers, stowage for the crew's Diemarco C8A1 carbines on the turret, a searchlight next to the gunner's sight on the turret roof, and an uparmoured commander's sight. Latterly, Leopard 2A5DK have been fitted with new Diehl 570PO tracks.

In 2007 Denmark decided to send four tanks of the Danish Quick Reaction Force (QRF) to Afghanistan as part of ISAF's mission there. A number of changes were introduced for the Leopard 2A5DKs deployed to Afghanistan from 2007 until 2014. These included the Barrucuda Mobile Camouflage System, protected optics, a turret-mounted wire cutter, and slat armour. At least twelve separate tanks were flown out to Afghanistan during the course of the Danish mission there. The first Leopard 2A7 vehicle was officially handed over by KMW to the Danish Army on 1 November 2019. The first of the new Leopard 2A7DK vehicles arrived at the barracks of the Jutland Dragoon Regiment in February 2020. The aim is for Denmark to receive 44 vehicles by 2022.

Tank 68.622 from the Jutland Dragoon Regiment is a veteran from Afghanistan, indicated by the brackets for the slat armour on the turret, next to and below the vehicle number. Also the reinforced lower hull armour is evident. Note the worn appearance of the road wheels and the missing armour panels on the side skirts. (Thomas Antonsen)

A Leopard 2A4 FIN drives through Lahti during a military parade in December 2005. The additional handrail and turret stowage bin are evident, as are the cut outs in the side skirts. (Finnish Defence Forces)

FINLAND

In August 2002 Finland signed a contract to replace its ageing fleet of T-55s and T-72M1s with 124 Leopard 2A4 from ex-Bundeswehr stocks. By July 2003 121 had been delivered, with 100 being in active service and the remainder used as spares and as training vehicles. The tanks were largely unmodified vehicles of the first to sixth production batches, all to 2A4 specifications. A number of small changes took place once they been adopted by the Finnish Army: anti-slip coating was added to the hull and turret roof, an additional stowage box was added to the turret front for snow grousers, while three stowage boxes were added to extend the turret rear. Extra cut-outs were also added for steps in the side skirts, US-style antennae mounts and another handrail on the turret front, while the flag pole mount on the right side of the turret was removed. Most notably, the Leopard 2A4 FIN received a distinctive three-colour splinter camouflage. In 2009 the Finns purchased another fifteen tanks from Germany to maintain the serviceability of their Leopard 2 fleet. As well as the gun tank, the Finns also employ the Leopard 2L Leguan Bridge Layer and the Leopard 2R Minefield Breaching Vehicle.

In January 2014 Finland announced a €200 million deal to purchase the remaining stock of 100 Leopard 2A6 tanks from the Netherlands. These were delivered over the course of the year and in 2015 the Leopard 2A4 FIN was withdrawn from frontline service. The Leopard 2A6 was received in its Dutch configuration (Dutch-style smoke dischargers and FN MAG loader's machine gun) and, initially at least, retained the standard three-colour NATO camouflage before being repainted in the Finnish splinter pattern. In peacetime the Finnish Leopard 2s are assigned to the Armoured Brigade, based in Parola, but would be divided into separate mechanised battlegroups in wartime.

A Finnish Leopard 2A6 during the 2016 Flag Day parade in Turku. The tank is still in Dutch NATO camouflage, but note the Finnish national marking. (MFKI)

The Leopard 2A4GR remains in service with the 21st Brigade of the Hellenic Army's 20th Armoured Division. This one was photographed during the Oxi Day Parade in 2018. (Fanis Boskos

GREECE

In 1998 the Greek army conducted field trials to select a new MBT from the American M1A2, the British Challenger 2, the French Leclerc, Russian T-80U, Ukrainian T-84 and the Leopard 2 in the guise of the Swedish Strv 122. The Leopard 2 was the clear winner and in 2003-2004 183 ex-Bundeswehr Leopard 2A4s were delivered to the Hellenic Army. They received a new camouflage scheme, similar to the old U.S. Army MERDC scheme. In 2005 work began on the development of a Leopard 2HEL, a tank to Leopard 2A6EX specifications. The Leopard 2HEL has a number of differences to the German tank: additional bow armour, increased roof protection with additional stowage boxes for camouflage net poles and small arms, a side turret stowage basket for the camouflage net, an enlarged turret rear with a cooling system, a crosswind sensor, APU on the rear right-hand hull, and additional handrails on the rear turret. It has also second-generation thermal sights (Ophelias) and the Iniochos command-and-information system. The first thirty vehicles were assembled in Germany, the remaining 140 in Greece. The Leopard 2HEL was accepted into service in March 2008.

A Leopard 2HEL of 25th Brigade, 20th Armoured Division, during Exercise Strike Back which took place on the Novo Selo Training Ground in Bulgaria in June 2019. (U.S. Army photo by Spc. Samantha Hall)

A Dutch Leopard 2NL.
(Nationaal Archief)

THE NETHERLANDS

The Royal Netherlands Army were the first export user of the German Leopard 2 after the Dutch government approved the purchase of 445 tanks in March 1979 following analysis of the results of the trials of the Leopard 2AV and US XM1 tanks. Indeed the Leopard 2 was developed with close cooperation between the Dutch and the Germans and at least one tank of the first-series production lot was delivered to the Dutch army for evaluation. This first-series tank was accepted in September 1981 and the Leopard 2NL equipped the 41 and 43 Tankbataljons from 1983. The next year another unit, 103 Verkenning (Armoured Reconnaissance) Bataljon, was equipped with the Leopard 2NL and the final vehicle was accepted into Dutch service in July 1986.

The Leopard 2NL was different to the German 2nd and 3rd production-series Leopard 2A1 in a number of ways. First, it

A Leopard 2NL during Exercise Free Lion in September 1988. Note the distinctive smoke grenade launchers on the turret side and the American-style aerials. (Echkhard Ude)

was equipped with RT3600 radios and had American-style S-style AS-1729 aerials on a MX-6707 base unit. The antenna tuning system also had a different access panel with a socket for the field telephone to the German Leopard. The commander's cupola-mounted MG3 was replaced with the FN 7.62mm MAG machine gun, while the side turret smoke launchers were replaced with the standard 3x2 launchers fitted to all Dutch AFVs. Between 1985 and 1987 the Leopard 2NLs were brought up to 2A4 standard with the fitting of the new digital ballistic processing unit. At this time the ammunition supply hatch on the left side of the turret was also welded shut on those vehicles that still had it operational and the Dutch Leopard 2s were fitted with the new uparmoured front side skirts. Unlike their German counterparts, however, they were not fitted with the new fire suppression system in the crew compartment (merely retaining the fire extinguishers).

The decision to upgrade the Leopard 2NLs to A5 standard was taken as early as March 1994, but the Leopard 2NL remained in service until 2002 when it had been fully replaced by the Leopard 2A5NL. With the end of the Cold War in the early 1990s 150 Leopard 2NLs were mothballed rather than being upgraded to A5 standard. In 1998 114 tanks were sold to Austria and later another 52 to Norway. As late as December 2007 the last remaining eighty Dutch Leopard 2A4NLs were sold to Canada.

The first Leopard 2A5NL was delivered to 42 Tankbataljon in May 1998. The Leopard 2A5NL retained all the details peculiar to the Leopard 2NL (smoke dischargers, FN MAG and different communications equipment), but in other respects had the same specifications the German Leopard 2A5, principally the wedge-shaped spaced turret armour which transformed the appearance of the tank. The second phase of upgrading the Leopard 2NL, due to take place between 2000 and 2002, was cancelled and, instead, all 180 Leopard 2A5NL tanks were upgraded with KWS I measures, principally the L/55 120mm smoothbore cannon, as Leopard 2A6NL. By 2004 all Dutch tanks were thus converted. The only other external difference between Dutch and German Leopard 2A6s was that the former retained the lighter pattern side skirts.

The Dutch Leopard 2 was designed to have played a pivotal role in the defence of West Germany as part of the NATO's Northern Army Group's I Netherlands Corps. In fact, it was not until NATO's operations in the Balkans as part of IFOR and SFOR that the Dutch tanks saw active service. In December 2007 the Dutch sold twenty Leopard 2A6NL to Canada and a further 37 to Portugal. In April 2011 the Dutch government announced that it would disband the final remaining armoured unit of the Royal Army and the following month the last round was fired by a Leopard 2A6NL at the Bergen Hohne Training Area in northern Germany. Plans to sell the remaining Dutch Leopards to Indonesia and Peru proved abortive, but in January 2014 the Dutch agreed to sell their remaining Leopard 2A6NL fleet to Finland. However, in September 2015, and as part of NATO's response to Russian aggression in Ukraine and the annexation of Crimea, the Dutch government announced they would take sixteen tanks out of stowage and lease a further eighteen from Germany to create a single tank squadron of eighteen Leopard 2A6M in the Royal Army. This now serves as part of the Bundeswehr's Panzerbataillon 414, part of the Dutch 43rd Mechanised Brigade.

A Leopard 2A6NL at the Dutch Cavalry Firing Range in Vlieland in March 2002. (NIHM Collectie Nederlands Instituut voor Militaire Historie)

A Leopard 2A4NO in its natural environment. The snow camouflage netting is a standard part of the Norwegian Leopard 2's equipment. (Soldatnytt).

NORWAY

Norway purchased 52 Leopard 2NLs from the Dutch in 2001 to replace its fleet of aging Leopard 1 MBTs which had been in service since the 1970s. The Dutch Leopard 2s were largely unmodified for Norwegian service. The Dutch-style smoke dischargers were replaced with the more widely used German version and, most importantly, a new Norwegian communications system (BMS) and a GPS system were added. This resulted in the Norwegian Leopard 2s having three rod antennae on the turret, as well as a cone antenna for the GPS. A large stowage bin was fitted to the rear of the turret, and the cable drum for the field telephone and deep wading equipment were also stowed on the turret rear. Norwegian Leopard 2s, however, retained the FN MAG on the loader's cupola. A distinctive feature of some Leopard 2A4NOs is the replacement of the heavy front section of the side skirts with the lighter ones fitted to the Leopard 1. From 2015 the Leopard 2A4, along with the Norwegian CV90 Infantry Fighting Vehicle, were upgraded with a digital Battlefield Management System.

Norway currently operates 36 Leopard 2A4NO. These are organised in two squadrons, one serving with the Panserbataljonen based in Setermoen and the other with the Telemark Bataljon in Rena, both part of Norway's principal combat formation, the Brigade Nord. The Norwegians are aware of the shortcomings of the Leopard 2A4NO, now in its fourth decade of service, and negotiations are ongoing about the possibility of leasing more modern vehicles from Germany.

Leopard 2A4NOs on the move near the Norwegian town of Engerdal during Exercise Trident Juncture 18. (Bundeswehr photo by SGM Marco Dorow)

A Polish Leopard 2A5 during the Strong Europe Tank Challenge in 2017. The four-digit tactical numbers are characteristic of the Leopard 2 in Polish service. (US Army photo by Sgt. Kathleeen Polanco)

POLAND

In July 1997 Poland was invited to join NATO and immediately began the process of acquiring NATO weapons systems to complement, and in some cases, replace its Soviet-era material. In September 2002 the first fifteen of 128 Leopard 2A4s were delivered to the 10th Armoured Cavalry Brigade of the Polish army. The vehicles were adopted in the standard configuration of German tanks and the Poles cooperated closely with the Bundeswehr to get to grips with their new mounts. The Leopard 2 is a very different prospect to the Warsaw Pact armour previously employed by the Poles and the Polish army is unique in operating the Leopard 2 alongside the PT-91 Twardy (Hard) MBT, a Polish-built version of the Soviet T-72M1.

In 2013 Germany and Poland signed a further agreement for the delivery of 105 Leopard 2A5s and a further 14 Leopard 2A4s. This took place between May 2014 and December 2015 and they currently serve with the 34th Armoured Cavalry Brigade. In the same month the Polish government signed a deal with Rheinmetall Landsystem to upgrade 128 Leopard 2A4PL to the new Leopard 2PL, with a further agreement for the remaining Leopard 2A4PLs in July 2018. This upgrade features new turret armour, new thermal imaging sights, a fire suppression system, and a rear view camera for the driver, bringing the entire Polish tank fleet to at least 2A5 standard. The first Leopard 2PLs were due to be delivered to active units in 2019.

A Leopard 2A4PL of the 15th Mechanised Brigade trains alongside Romanian troops as part of NATO Enhanced Forward Presence Battlegroup Poland in Bemowo Piskie, Poland, in February 2020. (US Army photo by Sgt. Timothy Hamlin)

The Dutch origins of Portugal's Leopard 2A6s are evident from the Dutch-style smoke dischargers and older-pattern side skirts. (Carlos Rocha)

PORTUGAL

Portugal was one of the twelve founding members of NATO back in 1949, but its armoured forces have traditionally been insignificant, even during the height of the Cold War. In the 1990 they acquired about 100 M60A3 TTS MBTs from the United States to replace their veteran M47 and M48 tanks. Portuguese troops served in NATO missions to the Balkans and Afghanistan, as well as in Iraq, but only infantry were deployed. The decision to acquire 37 Leopard 2A6 from the Netherlands in September 2007 was therefore something of a surprise. The first Leopard 2A6PRT were officially received at Constância in October the following year, with the delivery completed by the end of 2009. The tanks currently serve across three squadrons of the Grupo de Carros de Combate of the Portuguese Mechanised Brigade based in Santa Margarida barracks in Constância.

Portuguese Leopard 2A6s of the Multinational Brigade conduct manoeuvres in Santa Margarida during JOINTEX 15, part of NATO's Exercise Trident Juncture 15 in October 2015. (Allied Joint Force Command photo by Sgt Sébastien Fréchette)

SWEDEN

In the late 1980s Sweden decided to replace its fleet of Centurions and the home-designed S-Tank (Stridsvagn (Strv) 103). In 1994, following trials between the Leopard 2, Leclerc and M1A2 Abrams, the Swedes decided to procure the Leopard 2. The decision was, in part, affected by the availability of ex-Bundeswehr Leopard 2A4 and 160 of these were delivered between 1997 and 2001. In Swedish service they are known as the Strv 121. They were painted in a characteristic three-colour splinter camouflage and received a number of modifications. These included new radios and American-style antennae mounts, special rounded front mudguards, a reflector mounted on the front spare track bracket, and a tarpaulin cover the rear stowage box, while the rear-most trackguard was also cut away to prevent mud build up from the drive sprocket. Further modifications, including a rear view camera and infantry telephone, were added under the Strv 121B programme.

In October 1995 the first Strv 122, a Leopard 2 purpose built to A5 standards for the Swedes, was handed over by Krauss-Maffei to the Swedish armed forces. The first 29 tanks were built in Germany but thereafter, from spring 1998, production continued in Sweden. At the time the Strv 122 was the most potent Leopard 2 in service. Basically it was identical to the German Leopard 2A5 but had improved ballistic protection for the Peri sight, extra protection for the turret roof, French GALIX

(above) A Strv 121 of the Skaraborg Regiment photographed in 2005.

smoke dischargers, as well as an improved fire-control computer, a new air intake for the engine compartment, a tank/infantry phone at the rear of the vehicle, and an additional composite armour package that could be fitted to the tank's front hull. During the production run a digital GPS was introduced to support the Tank Command and Control System (TCCS) specially developed for the Strv 122.

In the second half of the 2000s the Strv 121 were retired from service and have been subsequently returned to Germany. Currently, the Swedish Army has 120 Strv 122 in service, divided between the Skaraborg, South Scanian and Norbotten regiments, each of whom field two companies of Strv 122. In 2016 the Swedes ordered an upgrade of their MBT fleet, with new Saab-designed commander's gunsight, a new computer system, Barracuda armour package for international deployments, and an active-protection system.

A good close up of a Strv 122, showing the GALIX smoke dischargers, during the Strong Europe Tank Challenge in 2018. (US Army photo by Gertrud Zach)

SPAIN

Spain began considering a replacement for its fleet of second-generation MBTs in the early 1980s, although political considerations demanded that the new tank be built in Spain. Working with Krauss-Maffei, the Spanish favoured the 'Lince', a shorter and lighter version of the Leopard 2, but amidst national political scandals and indecision, the project never materialised. It was not until 1995 that a memorandum of understanding was signed between the Spanish and German governments to deliver 108 Leopard 2A4 from Bundeswehr stocks to Spain for 16.9 million Euros. The tanks were delivered to Spain in 1998 without modifications apart from a new radio system. The existing M48s, M60s and AMX-30 MBTs were quickly retired from service and the first Leopard 2A4s were assigned to the XXIst Brigade, a unit earmarked for the putative Eurocorps based in Strasbourg.

At the same time as Spain signed its memorandum of understanding with the Germany, the Ejercito de Tierra (Spanish Army) launched its Programa Coraza – 2000 (Programme Armour 2000) aimed at modernising the country's armoured forces. The twin pillars of this were development of a new Leopard 2E and the Ascod/Pizarro Infantry Fighting Vehicle. The original order called for no fewer than 308 Leopard 2E with a price tag of 2.4 billion Euro which included the assembling of the MBTs by Spain's Santa Barbara Sistemas company using components mainly made in Spain. In fact only 219 Leopard 2Es were delivered, with the first thirty assembled at Krauss-Maffei Wegmann in Munich, before Barbara Sistemas was purchased by KMW's direct competitor General Dynamics in 2001. The Ejercito de Tierra's Leopard 2E is based on the Leopard 2A6EX, a tank which combines the Swedish Stridsvagn 122, with its roof add-on armour package, with the Auxiliary Power Unit of the Danish Leopard 2A5DK, albeit with a different engine-generator combination and the L/55 120mm smoothbore cannon of the Leopard 2A6. The tank also has the unique BMS LINCE (Leopard Information and Control Equipment), a modified version of the TCCS used on the Stridsvagn 122.

The Leopard 2E serves with four brigades: Brigada Acorazada 'Guadarrama' XII (Colmenar Viejo/Madrid), Brigada Acorazada 'Guzman El Bueno' X (CerroMuriano/Córdoba) and Brigada de Infanteria Mecanizada 'Extramadura' XI (Badajoz). The Leopard 2E is deployed as part of Spain's commitment to NATO's Enhanced Forward Presence as part of Battlegroup Latvia.

(below) A Leopard 2E is put through its paces on the Cerro Muriano training ground in Córdoba before its deployment to Latvia as part of NATO's Enhanced Forward Presence in 2017. (Stefan Degraef)

SWITZERLAND

Switzerland received 380 Leopard 2A4 between 1987 and 1993. These replaced the Centurions and the domestically produced Panzer 61 and Panzer 68 MBTs that had been in service since the 1960s. The procurement process had begun as long ago as 1979 and in 1981 two Leopard 2s had arrived in Switzerland for field trials. The Swiss army also trialled the US M1 Abrams the following year, but the German tank was considered superior in all regards. The first German-made tanks were handed over in the spring of 1987 and in December that year the first vehicles license-built in Switzerland were delivered. The Swiss renamed their Leopard 2s Panzer 87, with the contract completed by March 1993.

The Panzer 87 was basically the same as a fifth-series production Leopard 2A4. There were a number of minor changes: the coaxial and loader's MG3s were replaced by 7.5mm MG87s; four mounting brackets for spare MG barrels were fitted forward of the smoke dischargers on the turret sides; US AN/VCR radios and antennae replaced the German equipment; additional snow grousers were fitted on the front left and right sides of the turret; the turret rear corners were altered and a tank-infantry phone installed on the left side; a foldable storage rack for the camouflage net was fitted at the right rear of the turret; the headlights were modified to Swiss standards; a large sound suppressor was fitted to the exhausts at the hull rear; a hydraulic track tensioner and a modified NBC system was also fitted. During the production run the ammunition loading hatch on the left-hand side of the turret was welded shut and, from 120th vehicle produced in Switzerland, the new heavy-style side skirts were installed.

The Swiss opted out of the KWS II programme that would have seen their tanks upgraded to Leopard 2A5 standard and instead embarked upon their own Werterhaltungsprogramm from 2009 onwards. These introduced a number of improvements to the Leopard 87 fleet, including a new Peri RTW 17 sight for the commander, electronic gun control system (EWNA), rear-view camera for the driver, and a number of other electronic improvements and armour improvements. Originally 134 Panzer 87 were planned to be upgraded to Panzer 87 WE standard.

The Swiss army currently operates two tank battalions equipped with Panzer 87 WE, the Tank Battalion 12 (attached to Mechanised Brigade 1) and Tank Battalion 13 (attached to Mechanised Brigade 11).

(top) A Panzer 87 seen at a public display at Thun in 2006. Note the additional snow grousers fitted to the turret side and the stowage tubes for spare MG barrels. (Sandstein)

(left) Panzer 87 WE of Mechanised Brigade 11 on exercise in May 2018. (Swiss Army photo)

TURKEY

In the late 1990s Turkey decided to upgrade its extensive MBT fleet that consisted of M48s, M60s and almost 400 Leopard Is, a mixture of Leopard 1A1 to Leopard 1A4 variants and including 77 Leopard T1 tanks built especially for the Turkish army. In 1999 Turkey asked to conduct field trials with the Leopard 2A6EX, which proved successful, but opposition from the German Green Party, unhappy with Turkey's treatment of the Kurds, prevented the purchase of the latest generation of Leopard 2s. Instead, Ankara moved ahead with its decision to develop its own third-generation MBT, the Turkish National Battle Tank (TNMBT), which would be developed in cooperation with the South Korea. This led to the now infamous Altay MBT, one of the most expensive tanks in the world, which, despite a prototype being unveiled in 2016, is still to enter service (although serial production apparently started in 2018).

Given the delays to the TNMBT project, in 2005 the Turks procured 289 Leopard 2A4s from ex-Bundeswehr stocks. The first vehicles were delivered in the late summer of the following year. In fact, by 2014 a total of 342 Leopard 2A4s had been delivered to the Turkish army. All vehicles underwent a modernisation programme, installing a fire-control system manufactured by the Turkish company Aselsan. The only external difference to the Bundeswehr version of the Leopard 2A4, however, is the US-style antennae.

The Turkish Leopards serve among the armoured brigades of the Turkish army. Turkey has the second largest army in NATO, fielding some 2,500 MBTs, mainly M60A4 TTS Sabra and M48s. As we will see, the Leopard 2A4TU had an uncomfortable baptism of fire against ISIS during Operation Euphrates Shield in December 2016. Nevertheless, it remains one of the most powerful weapons in the Turkish arsenal.

(above) A Leopard 2A4TU of 2nd Armored Brigade during Operation Euphrates Shield in December 2016.

LEOPARD 2 IN COMBAT: BOSNIA AND KOSOVO

In December 1995 the presidents of Bosnia, Croatia and Serbia signed the Dayton Peace Accords, bringing an end to three-and-a-half years of vicious war in Bosnia. NATO's response was the deployment of IFOR (Implementation Force), a force of some 60,000 personnel organised into three multi-national divisions, to implement the agreement and protect the Bosnian civilian population from Serbian sectarian violence. Dutch Leopard 2A4s of the 11 Tankbataljon, one of the two remaining armoured battalions of the Regiment Huzaren van Sytzama (the other two, the 43rd and 49th, had been disbanded in 1992 and 1994), were deployed to Bosnia as part of IFOR. In 1997, under the auspices of the United Nations, the Dutch deployed the new Leopard 2A5NL as part of SFOR (Stabilisation Force) during Operation Joint Guard. The Dutch continued to serve in Bosnia after the termination of Operation Joint Guard in June 1998 under Operation Joint Forge (20 June 1998 until 2 December 2004).

While NATO's intervention in Bosnia was a peace-keeping mission, designed to keep the warring ethnic groups apart and implement a peace settlement, the situation the Alliance faced in Kosovo three years later was altogether more dangerous. In the summer of 1998 activities by the Kosovo Liberation Army (KLA) led to reprisals by the Yugoslavian and Serbian military, largely aimed against Kosovo's

(above) An IFOR Leopard 2NL of 11 Tankbataljon at Donji Barkuf in March 1996. (NIHM Collectie Nederlands Instituut voor Militaire Historie)

(below) An SFOR Leopard 2NL in camp at Banja Luka, Bosnia, as part of SFOR, in 1997. (NIHM Collectie Nederlands Instituut voor Militaire Historie)

An SFOR Leopard 2NL amidst the Bosnian snow. Note the prominent SFOR marking on the turret side. (Peter van Iren)

Albanian muslim population. In October NATO launched limited airstrikes against Yugoslav targets, but the fighting in Kosovo, and the atrocities, intensified. The failure of peace talks led to a much more sustained and intense NATO air campaign, which lasted from March until June 1999. On 10 June NATO suspended its air campaign when Yugoslavia agreed to withdraw from Kosovo and two days later NATO's Kosovo Force (KFOR) arrived to separate the warring parties and enforce peace in Operation Joint Guardian. As part of KFOR 28 Leopard 2A5 from the Bundeswehr's Panzerbataillonen 33 and 214 were deployed to the Balkans. The tanks saw

no action as such, although on 26 June a Leopard 2A5 fired four warning rounds from its main gun over the village of Orahovac. The nature of the terrain restricted the movement of heavy armour and the German MBTs were largely restricted to their base at Prizren. The following year they were replaced by Leopard 2A4. The Bundeswehr also deployed Leopard 2A4 to protect the German logistic base at Tetovo, Macedonia, in March 2001 amidst rising tensions between Albanian separatists and their Macedonian neighbours. Once tensions had lessened the tanks were redeployed to Camp Casablanca in Suva Reka, Kosovo, until their return to Germany in 2004.

A great overhead view of a SFOR Leopard 2NL. (Peter van Iren)

A Leopard 2A6M CAN moves onto the highway in Kandahar Province. (Canadian Combat Camera)

LEOPARD 2 IN COMBAT: AFGHANISTAN

In 2006 Canada deployed the first Main Battle Tanks to Afghanistan in support of ISAF'S operations in Kandahar Province. Fifteen Leopard C2s, a modified version of the Leopard 1A5, as well as an armoured recovery platoon, served in support of armoured infantry in Operation Medusa in the rural area west of Kandahar. On 16 August the following year, following requests from commanders in the field, the first of the newly procured Leopard 2A6M CAN arrived in Afghanistan. The Canadian tanks of Task Force Kandahar were operated by the soldiers of Lord Strathcona's Horse (Royal Canadians) until the final rotation of Canadian troops in Afghanistan (October 2010 – July 2011) when they were replaced by 12e Régiment blindé du Canada. Throughout their deployment to Afghanistan the Canadians maintained a troop of four Leopard 2A6M CAN at one of the Forward Operating Bases

(FOB) as a Reserve and Quick Reaction Force. In some circumstances the Leopard C2 was preferred over the Leopard 2 as the latter could not yet be fitted with the Track Width Mine Plough (TWMP), an essential piece of kit necessary to combat the biggest threat to Canadian troops in Kandahar, mines and IEDs.

Kandahar proved a tough environment for the Canadian tankers and their mounts. One challenge was the weather. The tanks were not equipped with air-conditioning units so instead the crews were issued with vests that circulated water cooled by the tank's chiller unit. The Barracuda MCS also helped to reduce the unbearable temperatures within the tank. Tank crews were also permitted to wear Air Force flight suits both for comfort and practicality. The other problem was that rain quickly made the sandy terrain treacherous for the heavier Leopard 2s, forcing them onto existing tracks. The Taliban were able to exploit this

Leopard 2A4M CAN and LAV III armoured vehicles prepare to leave Kandahar province at the end of the 10th Rotation of Canadian forces in July 2011. (Canadian Combat Camera)

to their advantage. On 28 March 2008, for example, a Leopard 2A6M CAN commanded by Lieutenant James Anderson drove over an insurgent IED. The ensuing explosion snapped the tank's torsion bars and blow the right leg off the driver, Corporal Mark Fuchko. With almost-superhuman effort, Fuchko managed to apply two tourniquets to his shattered limbs to prevent himself from bleeding to death. Nevertheless, the 120mm gun of the Leopard 2 proved itself indispensable, as did the rotating commander's independent thermal sight, a feature lacking in the Leopard C2. One tank commander, Warrant Officer Marvin Craig MacNeill, recalled firing a HEAT (High Explosive Anti-Tank) round at an insurgent position in the summer of 2008: the eleven hundred tungsten balls contained in the canister made a perfect circle in the vegetation between the Canadians and the insurgents and, when the dust cleared, 'the insurgent threat had been neutralised and the only identifiable piece of remains around the area was a sandal.'

On 25 October 2007 the first Danish Leopard 2 arrived in theatre to support ISAF's operations in Helmand Province. Four Leopard 2A5DK of the Quick Reaction Force (QRF), made up from the second squadron, 1st Armoured Batallion, the Jutland Dragoons Regiment, were deployed to Camp Bastion from where they moved to FOB Sandford to support British and Danish troops. Often the presence of the Danish tanks was sufficient to deter the Taliban from attacking ISAF troops, but the account of a battle fought on 5 January 2008 gives some sense of the combat experienced by the Danish Tank Detachment (TANKDET). During a two-hour long engagement the Leopard 2s fired 25 HEAT rounds at insurgent positions and troop concentrations, were fired upon by RPGs and helped identify Taliban positions for Allied airstrikes. Some of the fighting was at close quarters, with the Danish Leopard 2s engaging Taliban fighters at ranges of less than 300m. On 25 July 2008 the TANKDET suffered its one fatality of its deployment to Afghanistan. A tank drove over an IED, instantly killing the driver, Jesper Gilbert Pederson. The tank continued to move forward under its own power and the remaining crew members threw themselves from the tank before it came to a halt in a wadi. Unlike in the Leopard 2A6M CAN where it was slung in a hammock-style seat, the driver's position in the Leopard 2A5DK was bolted to the floor. Unfortunately in this case the blast occurred directly under the driver's escape hatch in the hull floor. On other occasions the Leopard 2A5DK proved capable of meeting the IED threat. On 2 April 2011 another tank was hit by an IED of around 45kg of homemade explosive. This bast broke a track and removed some of the sideskirt, but, apart from the commander who hit his head on the turret hatch, all the crew were unharmed. Indeed there was only tanker killed out of 43 fatalities suffered by the Danish ISAF contingent between 2008 and 2014. As one Danish tank commander observed: 'the value of having the Leopard tanks in Helmand was at least two-fold. Often, when the tanks were in the vicinity of Taliban insurgents, they simply chose not to fight. They knew they had no real way of fighting the tanks and, if they did, they would be under fire from a weapons platform which could engage them from far away, day or night. No other weapons platform in service with the entire Danish Armed Forces could provide this degree of safety for infantry soldiers on the ground.'

A Leopard 2A5DK crosses a bridge over Helmand River in Gereshk in 2012 while infantry stop the civilian traffic. (Danish Defence Command)

LEOPARD 2 IN COMBAT: SYRIA

The Syrian Civil War began in March 2011. It grew out of popular discontent with the Assad regime, but soon developed into an international conflict involving Syria's allies Iran and Russia and a host of Jihadist groups, most notably the so-called Islamic State (ISIS). In August 2016 Turkey, alarmed by both the advance of ISIS and the threat posed to Turkish security by the Syrian Democratic Forces (SDF) and the various Syrian Kurdish groups allied to the Kurdistan Workers' Party (PKK), invaded northern Syria. In December the Turkish army, with the assistance of their Syrian rebel allies (the Free Syrian Army – FSA), attempted to wrest control of the town of al-Bab from ISIS. At least a battalion-sized force of Leopard 2s were involved in this action. The performance of the Leopard 2s grabbed international attention and film of ISIS fighters examining knocked-out Turkish tanks led to headlines questioning the effectiveness of the MBT. The best-documented action, which led to the destruction of at least eight Leopard 2A4s, occurred around al-Bab hospital. How the tanks were knocked out was unclear in most cases, but vehicle-borne Improvised Explosive Devices (IEDs), mortar/rocket fire and ATGMs were all involved. Some

Leopard 2s may have been abandoned and subsequently destroyed by Turkish airstrikes. The battle for al-Bab (which fell to Turkey and its allies in February 2017) was the most widely reported loss of Leopard 2s in action, but Turkish MBTs continued to fall to the Kurdish People's Protection Units (YPG) and other groups throughout Operation Euphrates Shield. In February 2018, for instance, the YPG shared a video on YouTube showing a Leopard 2A4 being knocked out by an ATGM which hit the side of the tank and set off the ammunition stored inside. This prompted one Russian commentator to refer to the Leopard 2A4 as a 'bomb on caterpillars'. In January 2019 negotiations between Turkey and the German government over the release of political prisoners in return for an upgrade to the Turkish Leopard 2 fleet broke down amidst German media outrage over the use of Leopard 2s against Kurdish fighters in Afrin and Manbij. Turkey continues to use Leopard 2s in its operations in northern Syria, mainly as long-range fire support in exposed firing positions instead of being employed as part of a combined arms operation supported by infantry. Indeed, it is tactics used, rather than any inherent weakness in the tank itself, that has contributed to their indifferent combat performance.

Leopard 2A4s of Turkish 2nd Armoured Brigade in positions near al-Bab in the winter of 2016/17.

Turkish Leopard 2A4s on the move somewhere in northern Syria.

Further Reading

The most accessible introduction to the early development and history of the Leopard 2 Main Battle Tank remains M Jerchel's and U Schnellbacher, *Leopard 2 Main Battle Tank 1979-1998* (Osprey New Vanguard 24, 1998). This is now over twenty years old, so for the definitive account of the subsequent development and modernisation of the Leopard 2 the best place to start is with the work of Ralph Zwilling: *Leopard 2A4 Parts 1 and 2* (Tankograd Publishing Militärfahrzeug Spezial 5083, 5084, 2020), *Leopard 2A5 Parts 1 and 2* (Tankograd Publishing Militärfahrzeug Spezial 5075, 5076, 2018), *Leopard 2A6 Parts 1 and 2* (Tankograd Publishing Militärfahrzeug Spezial 5070, 5071, 2017), and *Leopard 2A7 2* (Tankograd Publishing Militärfahrzeug Spezial 5058, 2015). These are a wonderful resource of technical information, scale drawings and photographs.

Now sadly out of print, Frank Lobitz's two volumes on the Leopard 2 are also required reading. The second volume, in particular, is essential for anyone tackling a Leopard 2 in service outside the Bundeswehr: *Kampfpanzer Leopard 2: Entwicklung und Einsatz in der Bundeswehr* (Tankograd Publishing, 2009) and *Kampfpanzer Leopard 2: Internationaler Einsatz und Varianten* (Tankograd Publishing, 2009).

Tankograd Publishing have published a range of superb photo albums covering the tank in both Bundeswehr and foreign service.

Walter Böhm, *Leopard 2: The Leopard 2 MBT's Baptism of Fire on Army Exercises 1984-86* (Militärfahrzeug Spezial 5082, 2019)

Andreas Kirchoff, *Finnish Leopards* (International Special 8005, 2015)

Clement Niesner, *Svenska Armén: Vehicles of the Modern Swedish Army* (Missions & Manoeuvres 7027, 2015)

Daniel Nowak & Tom Mätzon, *10 Brygada Kawalerii Pancernej* (Missions & Manoeuvres 7025, 2014)

Daniel Nowak & Ralph Zwilling, *Panzer Task Force (*Militärfahrzeug Spezial 5069, 2017)

Carl Schulze, *Canadian Leopard 2A6M CAN* (International Special 8002, 2014)

Carl Schulze, *Leopard 2A4M CAN* (Fast Track 17, 2015)

Carl Schulze, *DANCON-ISAF: Danish Battle Group* (Missions & Manoeuvres 7024, 2014)

Jochen Vollert, *Leopard 2 Maintenance* (In Detail, 2013)

Ralph Zwilling, *Leopard 2A4: Kalter Krieger* (In Detail 2015)

Ralph Zwilling, *Panzer Brigade Bundeswehr* (Panzer Manöver 02, 2018)

Raph Zwilling, *Urbanes Panzergefecht Bundeswehr* (Panzer Manöver 03, 2018)

Trackpad Publishing also publish a great selection of Leopard-related titles, including some unique insights into the Leopard 2's service in Afghanistan:

Thomas Antonsen, *Danish Leopards in Helmand: from the Crew's Perspective* (Trackpad Publishing, 2017)

Kim Hartvig Sørensen, *Leopard 2A5DK in Afghanistan* (Trackpad Publishing, 2020)

Dan Hay, Peter van Iren, Anthony Sewards and Matthew Worth, *Leopard 2A4M CAN* (Trackpad Publishing, 2016)

Marvin Craig MacNeill, *They Called Us ... The New Evil: Memories from Afghanistan 2006-2008* (Trackpad Publishing, 2018)

Bobber Moller and Carl Schulze, *Danish Leopard 2A5DK...and QRF* (Trackpad Publishing, 2017)

Anthony Sewards and Rick Saucier, *Leopard 2A6M CAN in Afghanistan* (Trackpad Publishing, 2015)

There are several other books, mainly photo albums, that will provide inspiration for modellers:

Thomas Antonsen, *The Danish Leopard 2A5DK* (Barbarossa Books, 2009)

Walter Böhm, L*eopard 2/2A5* (Concord Mini Color Series 7501, 2004)

Chris Mrosko, *Dutch Leopard 2A4* (Sabot Publications Foto File 4, 2017)

Hermann Rössler and Hans Köhler, *Kampfpanzer Leopard 2: Der Beste der Welt* (Waffen Arsenal 69, 1981)

Michael Scheibert, *Leopard 2A5* (Waffen Arsenal Special 17, 1996)

My special gratitude to Michael Shackleton and Ralph Zwilling for their unfailing support in this project. Thanks are also due to Mark Smith, Thomas Antonsen, Fanis Boskos, Imad Bouantoun, Stefan de Graef, Peter van Iren, Chris Jerrett, Lester Plaskitt, M.P Robinson, Anthony Sewards and Slawomir Zajackowski for contributing ideas, photographs and models to this volume. This volume would not have been possible without the support of the Defense Visual Information Distribution Service (DVIDS), the Canadian Department of National Defence and the Netherlands Institute for Military History.

A Leopard 2A5NL of 42 Tankbataljon of the Prince of Orange's Hussars Regiment takes up position on a field training exercise in Germany in 2000. (NIHM Collectie Nederlands Instituut voor Militaire Historie)